50 *Fabulous*

Thread Crochet Edgings

by Susan Lowman

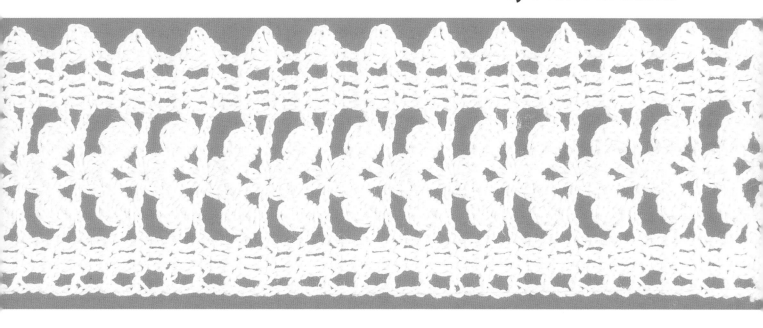

Leisure Arts, Inc.

Maumelle, Arkansas

Produced by

Production Team

Creative Directors: Jean Leinhauser
and Rita Weiss

Technical Editor: Ellen W. Liberles

Photographer: Carol Wilson Mansfield

Pattern Tester: Susan Jeffers

Book Design: Linda Causee

Published by Leisure Arts

©2014 by Leisure Arts, Inc.,
104 Champs Blvd., STE. 100
Maumelle, AR 72113 - 6738
www.leisurearts.com

Library of Congress Control Number: 2014948989

ISBN-13: 978-1-60900-400-2

Introduction

Have you ever completed a thread crochet project and thought something was missing? Or, have you planned to make a project you found online or in your favorite magazine, but felt something was needed that would make the project complete?

The answer is a simple one: add a decorative edging. An edging is actually really fun and easy to make. It can be the final touch that turns a simple thread project into something that is truly fabulous.

The edgings in this book are worked in one of two different ways: horizontally or vertically. If worked horizontally, the edging is worked in long rows along the edge of the desired piece or with the bottom edge of the edging attached to the edge of the desired piece after finishing. If worked vertically, the edging is worked in short rows, attaching one edge of the rows to the desired piece. The horizontal edgings will include a chain multiple for working the foundation chain in the pattern. The "chain multiple" will be given like this:

Chain multiple: 8 + 4

A chain multiple is the number of chain stitches needed to work one complete unit (or repeat) of a pattern. In the example (8 + 4), to work the pattern, you need to chain any number of stitches which can be divided evenly by 8 (the first number in the chain multiple): 16, 24, 32, 40, etc. To this number you need to add 4 more chains (the second number in the chain multiple), giving a total of 20, 28, 36, 44, etc. The "plus" (second) number is added just once, whereas the first number is the only number that is multiplied. This is the "formula" for making your foundation chain for the edging pattern. In this example, the instructions will begin like this:

Chain a multiple of 8 chains plus 4 additional chains.

All of the edgings in this book can be crocheted first, then attached to the edge of the desired piece when they are complete. Or they can be crocheted right onto the desired piece. It is your choice. If crocheting directly onto a piece of fabric or crochet, you have several choices. You can work single crochet directly onto the edge of the piece to replace the foundation chains of the edging. Or you can sew a blanket stitch around the edges of the piece first, then work single crochet into the blanket stitch to replace the foundation chains of the edging. If you crochet the edging first, you can then attach the edging with matching sewing thread or with the same crochet thread that you used to crochet the edging itself.

Once you start crocheting edgings, you'll find many places that need that extra bit of charm that only a fabulous thread edging can offer.

Contents

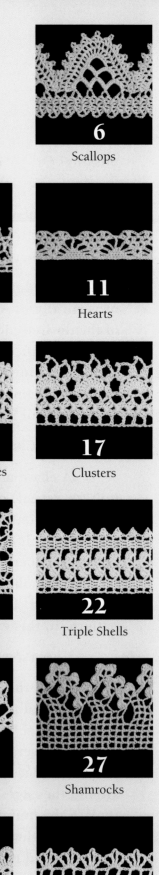

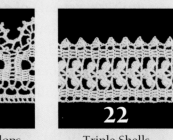

33

Pinecones

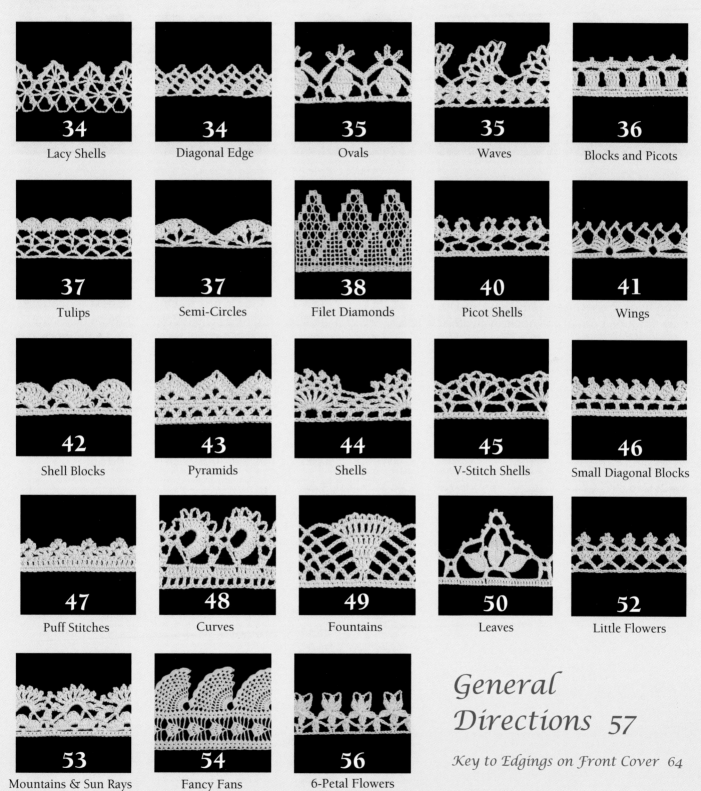

34

Lacy Shells

34

Diagonal Edge

35

Ovals

35

Waves

36

Blocks and Picots

37

Tulips

37

Semi-Circles

38

Filet Diamonds

40

Picot Shells

41

Wings

42

Shell Blocks

43

Pyramids

44

Shells

45

V-Stitch Shells

46

Small Diagonal Blocks

47

Puff Stitches

48

Curves

49

Fountains

50

Leaves

52

Little Flowers

53

Mountains & Sun Rays

54

Fancy Fans

56

6-Petal Flowers

General Directions 57

Key to Edgings on Front Cover 64

Scallops

Picot: Ch 5, sc in top of last dc worked before ch-5: picot made.

To join with sc: Make slip knot and place on hook, insert hook in specified st and draw up a lp, YO and draw through both lps on hook: join with sc made.

Instructions

Tape

Chain 8.

Row 1 (right side): (Dc, ch 1, dc) in 6th ch from hook, ch 1, 2 dc in next ch, ch 1, (dc, ch 1, dc) in last ch: 6 dc, 4 ch-1 sps and 1 ch-5 sp; ch 5, turn.

Row 2: Skip ch-5 sp and first ch-1 sp; *(dc, ch 1, dc, ch 1, dc) in next ch-1 sp; rep from * once; ch 5, turn.

Rows 3 through 10: Rep Row 2, 8 more times. At end of last row, ch 4 (instead of ch 5). Do NOT turn.

First Scallop

Row 1 (wrong side): Rotate piece to work along side edge; sc in first ch-5 sp, (ch 8, sc in next ch-5 sp) 3 times: 3 ch-8 sps and 1 ch-4 sp; turn.

Row 2: Work 12 sc in each of first 2 ch-8 sps, 6 sc in last ch-8 sp: 30 sc; turn.

Row 3: (Ch 8, sl st in 6th sc of next group of 12 sc) twice: 2 ch-8 sps; turn.

Row 4: Work 12 sc in first ch-8 sp, 6 sc in next ch-8 sp: 18 sc; turn.

Row 5: Ch 8, sl st in 6th sc of next group of 12 sc: 1 ch-8 sp; turn.

Row 6: Work 12 sc in ch-8 sp, 6 sc in each of next 2 partially worked ch-8 sps (on Rows 3 and 1): 24 sc; ch 3 (counts as dc on next row), sl st in first ch-4 sp at end of last row worked on tape (before scallop), turn.

Row 7: Ch 1, dc in first sc, ch 1, dc in next sc, (ch 1, skip next sc, dc in next sc) 6 times, (ch 1, dc in next sc) 9 times, (ch 1, skip next sc, dc in next sc) 6 times, ch 1, dc in last sc: 25 dc and 24 ch-1 sps; sc in next ch-5 sp along side edge of tape, ch 4 (counts as dc and ch-1 sp on following row), turn.

Row 8: (Dc, ch 1, dc) in first ch-1 sp, (ch 1, dc in next ch-1 sp) 10 times, ch 1, (dc, ch 1, dc) in next ch-1 sp, (ch 1, dc in next ch-1 sp) 11 times, ch 1, (dc, ch 1, dc) in last ch-1 sp: 28 dc and 27 ch-1 sps. Do not turn.

Tape (continued)

Row 11: Ch 2, skip first ch-1 sp on last row of tape; *(dc, ch 1, dc, ch 1, dc) in next ch-1 sp; rep from * once: 6 dc and 5 ch-1 sps; ch 5, turn.

Rows 12 through 20: Work same as Rows 2 through 10 on tape.

Second Scallop

Rows 1 through 6: Work same as Rows 1 through 6 on first scallop.

Row 7: Ch 1, dc in first sc, ch 1, dc in next sc, (ch 1, skip next sc, dc in next sc) 6 times, (ch 1, dc in next sc) 9 times, (ch 1, skip next sc, dc in next sc) 6 times, ch 1, dc in last sc: 25 dc and 24 ch-1 sps; sc in ch-2 sp at beg of first row of tape worked before current scallop, ch 1, sc in first ch-1 sp on Row 8 of previous scallop, turn.

Row 8: (Dc, ch 1, dc) in first ch-1 sp on current scallop, (ch 1, dc in next ch-1 sp) 10 times, ch 1, (dc, ch 1, dc) in next ch-1 sp, (ch 1, dc in next ch-1 sp) 11 times, ch 1, (dc, ch 1, dc) in last ch-1 sp: 27 dc and 26 ch-1 sps. Do not turn.

Rep Rows 11 through 20 of tape and Rows 1 through 8 of Second Scallop for desired length.

Tape (continued)

Last Row: Work same as Row 11 on tape, but do not ch 5 at end. Finish off; weave in ends.

Picot Points

With right side facing, join with sc in beg ch-4 sp on Row 8 of First Scallop; *ch 1, (dc, picot, dc) in next ch-1 sp, ch 1, sc in next ch-1 sp**; rep from * to ** 11 more times across scallop; ch 1, sc in 2nd ch-1 sp on next scallop; ***rep from * to ** 11 times across next scallop; ch 1, sc in 2nd ch-1 sp on next scallop; rep from *** across each scallop to last scallop; rep from * to ** 12 times across last scallop. Finish off; weave in ends.

Flowers

CHAIN MULTIPLE: 18 + 2

STITCH GUIDE

Tr-cl (triple crochet cluster): *YO twice, insert hook in specified st or sp and draw up a lp, (YO and draw through 2 lps on hook) twice; rep from * 2 more times; YO and draw through all 4 lps on hook: tr-cl made.

Instructions

Ch a multiple of 18 chs plus 2 additional chs.

Row 1 (right side): Sc in 2nd ch from hook and in each rem ch across; ch 5 (counts as dc and ch-2 sp on following row), turn.

Row 2: Skip first 3 sc, dc in next sc; *ch 2, skip next 2 sc, dc in next sc; rep from * across; ch 1, turn.

Row 3: Sc in first dc, (2 sc in next ch-2 sp, sc in next dc) 3 times; *ch 14, sc in 3rd ch from hook, hdc in next ch, dc in next 7 chs, hdc in next ch, sc in last 2 chs** (leaf made), sl st in top of last sc made before leaf, ch 15, sc in 8th ch from hook and in next 7 chs (stem made),

sl st in top of same sc as last sl st; rep from * to ** once (leaf made); sl st in top of same sc as last sl st***, (2 sc in next ch-2 sp, sc in next dc) 6 times; rep from * across, ending last rep at ***; (2 sc in next ch-2 sp, sc in next dc) 2 times, 2 sc in turning ch-5 sp, sc in 3rd ch of turning ch-5 sp. Finish off; weave in ends.

Row 4: With wrong side facing, join with sl st in ch-sp at tip of first leaf, ch 3; *in ch-sp at tip of next stem, work [(tr-cl, ch 7) 3 times, tr-cl]**, ch 7; rep from * across, ending last rep at **; ch 3, sl st in ch-sp at tip of last leaf; ch 1, turn.

Row 5: Sc in ch-sp at tip of first leaf (on Row 3), 3 sc in next ch-3 sp; *skip next tr-cl, (sc, hdc, 5 dc, hdc, sc) in next ch-7 sp; rep from * 2 more times; skip next tr-cl**, 3 sc in next ch-7 sp; working around same ch-7 sp, sc in ch-sp at tip of next 2 leaves, 3 sc in same ch-7 sp; rep from * across, ending last repeat at **; 3 sc in last ch-3 sp, sc in ch-sp at tip of last leaf (on Row 3). Finish off; weave in ends.

Pineapples

CHAIN MULTIPLE: 24 + 23

STITCH GUIDE

Shell: Work (2 dc, ch 2, 2 dc) in specified st or sp: shell made.

Picot: Ch 3, sl st in top of last st made before ch-3: picot made.

Instructions

Ch a multiple of 24 chs plus 23 additional chs.

Foundation Row (right side): Sc in 2nd ch from hook and in each rem ch across. Finish off.

Note: *Pineapples are worked one at a time along foundation row.*

First Pineapple

Row 1 (right side): With right side facing, join with sc in first sc, (ch 3, skip next 2 sc, sc in next sc) 7 times: 7 ch-3 sps; ch 5, turn, leaving rem sc unworked.

Row 2: Shell in first ch-3 sp, ch 4, skip next 2 ch-3 sps, [(tr, ch 1) 7 times, tr] in next ch-3 sp, ch 4, skip next 2 ch-3 sps, shell in last ch-3 sp, ch 5, sl st in next sc: 2 shells and 8 tr; ch 1, turn.

Row 3: Work 7 sc in first ch-5 sp, ch 1, shell in ch-2 sp of first shell, ch 3, skip next ch-4 sp, sc in next ch-1 sp, (ch 3, sc in next ch-1 sp) 6 times, ch 3, skip next ch-4 sp, shell in ch-2 sp of next shell: 2 shells and 8 ch-3 sps; ch 5, turn.

Row 4: Shell in ch-2 sp of first shell, ch 3, skip next ch-3 sp, sc in next ch-3 sp, (ch 3, sc in next ch-3 sp) 5 times, ch 3, skip next ch-3 sp, shell in ch-2 sp of next shell, ch 5, sl st in ch-1 sp: 2 shells and 7 ch-3 sps; ch 1, turn.

Row 5: Work 7 sc in first ch-5 sp, ch 1, shell in ch-2 sp of first shell, ch 3, skip next ch-3 sp, sc in next ch-3 sp, (ch 3, sc in next ch-3 sp) 4 times, ch 3, skip next ch-3 sp, shell in ch-2 sp of next shell: 2 shells and 6 ch-3 sps; ch 5, turn.

Row 6: Shell in ch-2 sp of first shell, ch 3, skip next ch-3 sp, sc in next ch-3 sp, (ch 3, sc in next ch-3 sp) 3 times, ch 3, skip next ch-3 sp, shell in ch-2 sp of next shell, ch 5, sl st in ch-1 sp: 2 shells and 5 ch-3 sps; ch 1, turn.

Row 7: Work 7 sc in first ch-5 sp, ch 1, shell in ch-2 sp of first shell, ch 3, skip next ch-3 sp, sc in next ch-3 sp, (ch 3, sc in next ch-3 sp) 2 times, ch 3, skip next ch-3 sp, shell in ch-2 sp of next shell: 2 shells and 4 ch-3 sps; ch 5, turn.

Row 8: Shell in ch-2 sp of first shell, ch 3, skip next ch-3 sp, sc in next ch-3 sp, ch 3, sc in next ch-3 sp, ch 3, skip next ch-3 sp, shell in ch-2 sp of next shell, ch 5, sl st in ch-1 sp: 2 shells and 3 ch-3 sps; ch 1, turn.

Row 9: Work (4 sc, picot, 3 sc) in first ch-5 sp, ch 1, 4 dc in ch-2 sp of first shell, ch 2, skip next ch-3 sp, dc in next ch-3 sp, ch 2, skip next ch-3 sp, 4 dc in ch-2 sp of next shell: 9 dc and 1 picot; ch 5, turn.

Row 10: Skip first 4 dc, (tr, ch 5, tr) in next dc, ch 5, skip next 4 dc, sl st in ch-1 sp: 2 tr and 3 ch-5 sps; ch 1, turn.

Row 11: [Work (4 sc, picot, 3 sc) in next ch-5 sp] 3 times, ch 1, (4 sc, picot, 3 sc) in next ch-5 sp, [ch 1, 7 sc in next ch-5 sp] 3 times: 5 picots.

Second and Subsequent Pineapples

Row 1 (right side): Sl st in next 2 sc on foundation row, sc in next sc, (ch 3, skip next 2 sc, sc in next sc) 7 times: 7 ch-3 sps; ch 5, turn, leaving rem sc unworked.

Row 2: Work same as Row 2 on First Pineapple.

Row 3: Work 4 sc in first ch-5 sp, ch 1, drop lp from hook, draw dropped lp through 4th sc worked on ch-5 sp at beg of Row 2 of previous pineapple, 3 sc in same ch-5 sp on current pineapple, ch 1, shell in ch-2 sp of first shell, ch 3, skip next ch-4 sp, sc in next ch-1 sp, (ch 3, sc in next ch-1 sp) 6 times, ch 3, skip next ch-4 sp, shell in ch-2 sp of next shell: 2 shells and 8 ch-3 sps; ch 5, turn.

Rows 4 through 6: Work same as Rows 4 through 6 on First Pineapple.

Row 7 (Joining Row): Work 4 sc in first ch-5 sp, ch 5, drop lp from hook, draw dropped lp through 4th sc worked on ch-5 sp at beg of Row 6 of previous pineapple, (4 sc, picot, 3 sc) in ch-5 sp just made between pineapples, 3 sc in same ch-5 sp on current pineapple, ch 1, shell in ch-2 sp of first shell, ch 3, skip next ch-3 sp, sc in next ch-3 sp, (ch 3, sc in next ch-3 sp) 2 times, ch 3, skip next ch-3 sp, shell in ch-2 sp of next shell: 2 shells, 4 ch-3 sps and 1 picot; ch 5, turn.

Rows 8 through 11: Work same as Rows 8 through 11 on First Pineapple. At end of last row on last pineapple, finish off; weave in ends.

Crowns

CHAIN MULTIPLE: 24 + 2

STITCH GUIDE

Cl (cluster): (YO, insert hook in specified st and draw up a lp, YO and draw through 2 lps on hook) 3 times, YO and draw through all 4 lps on hook: Cl made.

Picot: Ch 4, sc in 4th ch from hook: picot made.

2-dc Cl (2 double crochet cluster): (YO, insert hook in specified st and draw up a lp, YO and draw through 2 lps on hook) 2 times, YO and draw through all 3 lps on hook: 2-dc Cl made.

Instructions

Ch a multiple of 24 chs plus 2 additional chs.

Row 1 (wrong side): Sc in 2nd ch from hook and in each rem ch across; ch 6, turn.

Row 2 (right side): Skip first 2 sc, sc in next sc; *ch 6, skip next 3 sc, sc in next sc; rep from * across to last 2 sc; ch 3, skip next sc, dc in last sc; ch 1, turn.

Row 3: Sc in first dc, ch 6, sc in next ch-6 sp; *ch 3, Cl in next sc, ch 3, sc in next ch-6 sp**, (ch 6, sc in next ch-6 sp) twice; rep from * across, ending last rep at **; ch 6, sc in 3rd ch of turning ch-6; ch 6, turn.

Row 4: Sc in first ch-6 sp; *ch 3, Cl in next sc, ch 3, sc in next Cl, (ch 6, sc in next ch-6 sp) twice, ch 6, sc in next Cl, ch 3, Cl in next sc, ch 3, sc in next ch-6 sp**, ch 6, sc in next ch-6 sp; rep from * across, ending last rep at **; ch 3, dc in last sc; ch 1, turn.

Row 5: Sc in first dc; *ch 3, Cl in next sc, ch 3, sc in next Cl, ch 6, sc in next ch-6 sp, 9 dc in next ch-6 sp, sc in next ch-6 sp, ch 6, sc in next Cl, ch 3, Cl in next sc, ch 3**, sc in next ch-6 sp; rep from * across, ending last rep at **; sc in 3rd ch of turning ch-6; ch 3, turn.

Row 6: Dc in first sc; *ch 3, sc in next Cl, 3 sc in next ch-3 sp, 3 sc in next ch-6 sp, ch 3, Cl in next dc, (ch 1, picot, ch 1, skip next dc, Cl in next dc) 4 times, ch 3, 3 sc in next ch-6 sp, 3 sc in next ch-3 sp, sc in next Cl, ch 3**, Cl in next sc; rep from * across, ending last rep at **; 2-dc Cl in last sc. Finish off; weave in ends.

Royalty

CHAIN MULTIPLE: 12 + 6

STITCH GUIDE

Picot: Ch 3, sl st in 3rd ch from hook: picot made.

Tr-cl (triple crochet cluster): *YO twice, insert hook in specified st or sp and draw up a lp, (YO and draw through 2 lps on hook) twice; rep from * 2 more times; YO and draw through all 4 lps on hook: tr-cl made.

Instructions

Ch a multiple of 12 chs plus 6 additional chs.

Row 1 (right side): Dc in 7th ch from hook; *ch 2, skip next 2 chs, dc in next ch; rep from * across to last 2 chs; ch 1, skip next ch, dc in last ch; ch 1, turn.

Row 2: Sc in first dc; *ch 5, skip next ch-2 sp, sc in next ch-2 sp; from from * across to last ch-2 sp; ch 5, skip last ch-2 sp, skip first ch of turning ch, sc in next ch of turning ch; ch 1, turn.

Row 3: Sc in first sc; *(2 sc, picot, 3 sc, picot, 2 sc) in next ch-5 sp; rep from * across to last sc; sc in last sc; ch 7 (counts as tr and ch-3 sp on following row), turn.

Row 4: Skip first picot, sc in center sc of 3 sc between picots; *ch 7, skip next 2 picots, sc in center sc of 3 sc between picots; rep from * across to last picot; ch 3, skip last picot, skip next 2 sc, tr in last sc; ch 1, turn.

Row 5: Sc in first tr; *ch 3, [(tr-cl, ch 3) 4 times] in next ch-7 sp**, sc in next ch-7 sp; rep from * across, ending last rep at **; sc in 4th ch of turning ch-7; ch 1, turn.

Row 6: Sc in first sc; *(sc in next ch-3 sp, ch 3) 4 times, sc in next ch-3 sp; rep from * across to last sc; sc in last sc; ch 1, turn.

Row 7: Sc in first sc; *ch 3, (sc in next ch-3 sp, ch 2, picot, ch 2) 3 times, sc in next ch-3 sp; rep from * across; ch 3, skip next sc, sc in last sc. Finish off; weave in ends.

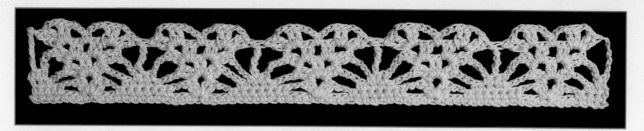

Hearts

CHAIN MULTIPLE: 14 + 2

STITCH GUIDE

Dtr (double triple crochet): YO 3 times, insert hook in specified st and draw up a lp, (YO and draw through 2 lps on hook) 4 times: dtr made.

Instructions

Ch a multiple of 14 chs plus 2 additional chs.

Row 1 (right side): Sc in 2nd ch from hook and in each rem ch across; ch 1, turn.

Row 2: Sc in first 4 sc; *ch 2, skip next 3 sc, (2 dc, ch 2, 2 dc) in next sc, ch 2, skip next 3 sc**, sc in next 7 sc; rep from * across, ending last rep at **; sc in last 4 sc; ch 1, turn.

Row 3: Sc in first 3 sc; *ch 3, skip next ch-2 sp, (2 dc, ch 2, 2 dc, ch 2, 2 dc) in next ch-2 sp, ch 3, skip next sc**, sc in next 5 sc; rep from * across, ending last rep at **; sc in last 3 sc; ch 1, turn.

Row 4: Sc in first 2 sc; *ch 4, skip next ch-3 sp, (2 dc, ch 2, 2 dc) in next ch-2 sp, ch 1, (2 dc, ch 2, 2 dc) in next ch-2 sp, ch 4, skip next sc**, sc in next 3 sc; rep from * across, ending last rep at **; sc in last 2 sc; ch 5 (counts as dtr on following row), turn.

Row 5: *Skip next ch-4 sp, (2 dc, ch 2, 2 dc) in next ch-2 sp, ch 3, sc in next ch-1 sp, ch 3, (2 dc, ch 2, 2 dc) in next ch-2 sp, skip next sc, dtr in next sc; rep from * across. Finish off; weave in ends.

Diagonal Blocks

STITCH GUIDE

Shell: Work (3 dc, ch 2, 3 dc) in specified st or sp.

Beg shell (beginning shell): Ch 3, (2 dc, ch 2, 3 dc) in same sp as joining sl st: beg shell made.

Large shell: Work (3 dc, ch 3, 3 dc) in specified st or sp.

Instructions

Ch 16.

Row 1 (wrong side): Work beg shell in 4th ch from hook, ch 9, skip next 11 chs, shell in last ch: 2 shells and 1 ch-9 sp; ch 5, turn.

Row 2 (right side): Shell in ch-sp of first shell, ch 11, shell in ch-sp of next shell, ch 2, skip next 2 dc of shell, dc in next ch: 2 shells, 1 ch-11 sp and 1 ch-2 sp; ch 5 (counts as dc and ch-2 sp on following row), turn.

Row 3: Skip first dc, dc in first dc of shell, ch 2, shell in ch-sp of same shell, ch 7, sc around all 3 ch-sps below, ch 1, turn; sc in each of 7 chs, (ch 1, turn; sc in back lp of next 7 sc) 5 times (block made); shell in ch-sp of next shell: 2 shells, 2 ch-2 sps and 1 block; ch 5, turn.

Row 4: Shell in ch-sp of first shell, ch 11, shell in ch-sp of next shell, ch 2, skip next 2 dc of same shell, dc in next dc, ch 2, dc in next dc, ch 2, skip next 2 chs, dc in next ch: 2 shells, 1 ch-11 sp and 3 ch-2 sps; ch 5 (counts as dc and ch-2 sp on following row), turn.

Row 5: Skip first dc, (dc in next dc, 2 dc in next ch-2 sp) twice, dc in first dc of shell, ch 2, shell in ch-sp of same shell, ch 9, shell in ch-sp of next shell: 2 shells, 1 ch-9 sp and 2 ch-2 sps; ch 5, turn.

Row 6: Shell in ch-sp of first shell, ch 11, shell in ch-sp of next shell, ch 2, skip next 2 dc of same shell, dc in next dc, ch 2, dc in next 7 dc, ch 2, skip next 2 chs, dc in next ch: 2 shells, 1 ch-11 sp and 3 ch-2 sps; ch 5 (counts as dc and ch-2 sp on following row), turn.

Row 7: Skip first dc, (dc in next dc, ch 2, skip next 2 dc) twice, (dc in next dc, 2 dc in next ch-2 sp) twice, dc in first dc of shell, ch 2, shell in ch-sp of same shell, ch 7, sc in tip of previous block (enclosing all 3 chains in st), ch 1, turn; sc in each of 7 chs just made, (ch 1, turn; sc in back lp of next 7 sc) 5 times (block made); shell in ch-sp of next shell: 2 shells, 4 ch-2 sps and 1 block; ch 5, turn.

Row 8: Shell in ch-sp of first shell, ch 11, shell in ch-sp of next shell, ch 2, skip next 2 dc of same shell, dc in next dc, ch 2, dc in next 7 dc, (ch 2, dc in next dc) twice, ch 2, skip next 2 chs, dc in next ch: 2 shells, 1 ch-11 sp and 5 ch-2 sps; ch 5 (counts as dc and ch-2 sp on following row), turn.

Row 9: Skip first dc, (dc in next dc, 2 dc in next ch-2 sp) twice, (dc in next dc, ch 2, skip next 2 dc) twice, (dc in next dc, 2 dc in next ch-2 sp) twice, dc in first dc of shell, ch 2, shell in ch-sp of same shell, ch 9, shell in ch-sp of next shell: 2 shells, 1 ch-9 sp and 4 ch-2 sps; ch 5, turn.

Row 10: Shell in ch-sp of first shell, ch 11, shell in ch-sp of next shell, ch 2, skip next 2 dc of same shell, dc in next dc, ch 2, dc in next 7 dc, (ch 2, dc in next dc) twice, dc in next 6 dc, ch 2, skip next 2 chs, dc in next ch: 2 shells, 1 ch-11 sp and 5 ch-2 sps; ch 5 (counts as dc and ch-2 sp on following row), turn.

Row 11: Skip first dc; *(dc in next dc, ch 2, skip next 2 dc) twice, (dc in next dc, ch 2) twice; rep from * once; dc in first dc of shell, ch 2, shell in ch-sp of same shell, ch 7, sc in tip of previous block (enclosing all 3 chains in st), ch 1, turn; sc in each of 7 chs, (ch 1, turn; sc in back lp of next 7 sc) 5 times (block made); shell in ch-sp of next shell: 2 shells, 10 ch-2 sps and 1 block; ch 5, turn.

Row 12: Shell in ch-sp of first shell, ch 11, shell in ch-sp of next shell, ch 2, skip next 2 dc of same shell, dc in next dc: 2 shells, 1 ch-11 sp and 1 ch-2 sp; ch 5 (counts as dc and ch-2 sp on following row); turn, leaving rem sts unworked.

Row 13: Dc in first dc of shell, ch 2, shell in ch-sp of same shell, ch 9, shell in ch-sp of next shell: 2 shells, 1 ch-9 sp and 2 ch-2 sps; ch 5, turn.

Row 14: Rep Row 4.

Row 15: Skip first dc, (dc in next dc, 2 dc in next ch-2 sp) twice, dc in first dc of shell, ch 2, shell in ch-sp of same shell, ch 7, sc in tip of previous block (working around all 3 ch-sps below), ch 1, turn; sc in each of 7 chs, (ch 1, turn; sc in back lp of next 7 sc) 5 times (block made); shell in ch-sp of next shell: 2 shells, 2 ch-2 sps and 1 block; ch 5, turn.

Row 16: Rep Row 6.

Row 17: Skip first dc, (dc in next dc, ch 2, skip next 2 dc) twice, (dc in next dc, 2 dc in next ch-2 sp) twice, dc in first dc of shell, ch 2, shell in ch-sp of same shell, ch 9, shell in ch-sp of next shell: 2 shells, 1 ch-9 sp and 4 ch-2 sps; ch 5, turn.

Row 18: Rep Row 8.

Row 19: Skip first dc, (dc in next dc, 2 dc in next ch-2 sp) twice, (dc in next dc, ch 2, skip next 2 dc) twice, (dc in next dc, 2 dc in next ch-2 sp) twice, dc in first dc of shell, ch 2, shell in ch-sp of same shell, ch 7, sc in tip of previous block (enclosing all 3 chains in st), ch 1, turn; sc in each of 7 chs, (ch 1, turn; sc in back lp of next 7 sc) 5 times (block made); shell in ch-sp of next shell: 2 shells, 4 ch-2 sps and 1 block; ch 5, turn.

Row 20: Rep Row 10.

Row 21: Skip first dc; *(dc in next dc, ch 2, skip next 2 dc) twice, (dc in next dc, ch 2) twice; rep from * once; dc in first dc of shell, ch 2, shell in ch-sp of same shell, ch 9, shell in ch-sp of next shell: 2 shells, 1 ch-9 sp and 10 ch-2 sps; ch 5, turn.

Rep Rows 2 through 21 for desired length, ending with a Row 20 rep.

Last Row: Skip first dc; *(dc in next dc, ch 2, skip next 2 dc) twice, (dc in next dc, ch 2) twice; rep from * once; dc in first dc of shell, ch 2, shell in ch-sp of same shell, ch 4, sc in tip of previous block (working around ch-sp below), ch 4, shell in ch-sp of next shell: 2 shells, 10 ch-2 sps and 2 ch-4 sps. Finish off; weave in ends.

Edge

Row 1 (wrong side): With wrong side facing, working in diagonal edge of rows, join with sl st in ch-5 sp at beg of Row 3, work beg shell, (skip next row, shell in edge of next row) 3 times; *skip next row, large shell in ch-5 sp at edge of next row (tip of diagonal edge); working in ch-2 sps across top of same row, (skip next ch-2 sp, shell in next ch-2 sp) 4 times, skip last ch-2 sp**, working along edge of next diagonal, (skip next row, shell in edge of next row) 4 times; rep from * across, ending last rep at **; turn.

Row 2 (right side): Sl st in first 3 dc of shell, (sl st, ch 1, sc) in ch-sp of same shell; *(10 dc in ch-sp of next shell) 3 times, 15 dc in ch-sp of large shell, (10 dc in ch-sp of next shell) 3 times**, (sc in ch-sp of next shell) twice; rep from * across, ending last rep at **; sc in ch-sp of last shell. Finish off; weave in ends.

Clovers

CHAIN MULTIPLE: 26 + 17

STITCH GUIDE

Shell: Work (sc, hdc, 11 dc, hdc, sc) in specified sp: shell made.

Large shell: Work (sc, hdc, 15 dc, hdc, sc) in specified sp: large shell made.

Picot: Ch 3, sl st in top of last st worked before ch-3: picot made.

To join with dtr: Make a slip knot and place on hook, YO 3 times, insert hook in specified st and draw up a lp, (YO and draw through 2 lps on hook) 4 times: join with dtr made.

Instructions

Ch a multiple of 26 chs plus 17 additional chs.

First Clover

Row 1 (right side): Sc in 2nd ch from hook and in next 7 chs, ch 10, sc in 5th ch from hook to form a ring: 1 ring; turn.

Row 2: In ring work (ch 8, sc, ch 9, sc, ch 8, sc): 1 ch-9 sp and 2 ch-8 sp2; ch 1, turn.

Row 3: Shell in next ch-8 sp, large shell in next ch-9 sp, shell in next ch-8 sp, sl st in ring, sc in rem 5 chs of ch-10, sc in next 6 chs of foundation ch: 1 large shell and 2 shells; turn.

Row 4: Working in sts on shells, dc in 4th st on first shell, (ch 2, skip next st, dc in next st) 4 times, dc in 4th st on large shell, (ch 2, skip next st, dc in next st) 2 times, ch 2, skip next st, (dc, ch 2, dc) in next st, (ch 2, skip next st, dc in next st) 3 times, dc in 4th st on last shell, (ch 2, skip next st, dc in next st) 4 times, skip next 5 sc worked in foundation ch, sl st in next sc: 15 ch-2 sps; ch 1, turn.

Row 5: Work 5 sc in first ch-2 sp, [(3 sc, picot, 2 sc) in next ch-2 sp] 13 times, 5 sc in last ch-2 sp: 13 picots.

Second Clover

Row 1 (right side): Sc in next 20 chs on foundation ch, ch 10, sc in 5th ch from hook to form a ring: 1 ring; turn.

Rows 2 through 4: Work same as Rows 2 through 4 on First Clover.

Row 5: Work 5 sc in first ch-2 sp, 3 sc in next ch-2 sp, ch 1, sl st in last picot worked on previous clover, ch 1, sl st in last sc worked on current clover (joined picot made), 2 sc in same ch-2 sp, 3 sc in next ch-2 sp, ch 1, sl st in next picot on previous clover, ch 1, sl st in last sc worked on current clover (joined picot made), 2 sc in same ch-2 sp, [(3 sc, picot, 2 sc) in next ch-2 sp] 11 times, 5 sc in last ch-2 sp: 11 picots and 2 joined picots.

Rep Second Clover across to last 2 chs, sc in last 2 chs. Finish off; weave in ends.

Bottom Edge

With right side facing and foundation ch at top, working in free lps on opposite side of foundation chs, join with dtr in 4th ch, ch 2, working in front of last dtr, dtr in first ch; *(ch 2, skip next 5 chs, dtr in next ch, ch 2, working in front of last dtr, dtr in 3rd skipped ch) twice**; (ch 2, skip next 6 chs, dtr in next ch, ch 2, working in front of last dtr, dtr in 4th skipped ch) twice; rep from * across, ending last rep at **. Finish off; weave in ends.

Regency

CHAIN MULTIPLE: 12 + 2

STITCH GUIDE

Tr-cl (triple crochet cluster): *YO twice, insert hook in specified st or sp and draw up a lp, (YO and draw through 2 lps on hook) twice; rep from * once; YO and draw through all 3 lps on hook: tr-cl made.

Trefoil: Ch 6, sl st in top of last st made before ch-6, ch 8, sl st in top of same st, ch 6, sl st in top of same st: trefoil made.

Instructions

Ch a multiple of 12 chs plus 2 additional chs.

Row 1 (right side): Sc in 2nd ch from hook; *ch 2, skip next 2 chs, sc in next ch; rep from * across; ch 5 (counts as dc and ch-2 sp on following row), turn.

Row 2: Skip first ch-2 sp, dc in next sc; *ch 2, skip next ch-2 sp, dc in next sc; rep from * across; ch 1, turn.

Row 3: Sc in first dc; *ch 2, skip next ch-2 sp, sc in next dc; rep from * across to turning ch; ch 2, skip next 2 chs, sc in 3rd ch of turning ch-5; ch 6 (counts as dc and ch-3 sp on following row), turn.

Row 4: Skip first ch-2 sp, sc in next sc; *ch 7, skip next 2 ch-2 sps, sc in next sc; rep from * across to last ch-2 sp; ch 3, skip last ch-2 sp, dc in last sc; ch 1, turn.

Row 5: Sc in first dc, 2 sc in next ch-3 sp; *ch 2, (dc, ch 5, dc) in next ch-7 sp, ch 2**, 5 sc in next ch-7 sp; rep from * across, ending last rep at **; 2 sc in turning ch-sp, sc in 3rd ch of turning ch-6; ch 1, turn.

Row 6: Sc in first sc; *ch 4, skip next ch-2 sp, [(tr-cl, ch 3) 3 times, tr-cl] in next ch-5 sp, ch 4, skip next ch-2 sp, skip next 2 sc, sc in next sc; rep from * across; ch 4, turn.

Row 7: *Sc in next ch-4 sp, **sc in next tr-cl, 3 sc in next ch-3 sp, sc in next tr-cl***, (2 sc, trefoil, 2 sc) in next ch-3 sp; rep from ** to *** once; sc in next ch-4 sp; rep from * across; ch 4, sl st in last sc. Finish off; weave in ends.

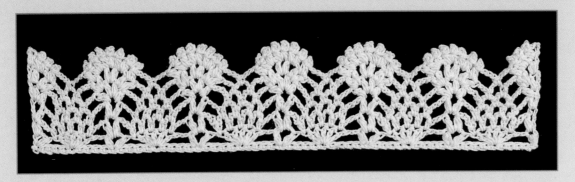

Puffs and Pineapples

CHAIN MULTIPLE: 10 + 2

STITCH GUIDE

Puff st (puff stitch): (YO, insert hook in specified st or sp and draw up a lp to height of current row) twice, YO and draw through all 5 lps on hook: puff st made.

Picot: Ch 3, sl st in top of last st made before ch-3: picot made.

Instructions

Ch a multiple of 10 chs plus 2 additional chs.

Row 1 (right side): Sc in 2nd ch from hook and in each rem ch across; ch 3 (counts as dc on following row now and throughout), turn.

Row 2: Puff st in first sc; *ch 1, skip next 4 sc, 5 dc in next sc, ch 1, skip next 4 sc**, (puff st, ch 2, puff st) in next sc; rep from * across, ending last rep at **; (puff st, dc) in last sc; ch 3, turn.

Row 3: Puff st in first dc; *ch 3, (sc in next dc, ch 3) 5 times**, (puff st, ch 2, puff st) in next ch-2 sp; rep from * across, ending last rep at **; (puff st, dc) in top of turning ch; ch 4 (counts as dc and ch-1 sp on following row), turn.

Row 4: Puff st in first dc; *ch 3, skip next ch-3 sp, (sc in next ch-3 sp, ch 3) 4 times, skip next ch-3 sp**, (puff st, ch 3, puff st) in next ch-2 sp; rep from * across, ending last rep at **; (puff st, ch 1, dc) in top of turning ch; ch 3, turn.

Row 5: Puff st in first dc, ch 1, puff st in next ch-1 sp; *ch 3, skip next ch-3 sp, (sc in next ch-3 sp, ch 3) 3 times, skip next ch-3 sp**, [(puff st, ch 1) 3 times, puff st] in next ch-3 sp (between puff sts); rep from * across, ending last rep at **; puff st in next ch-1 sp, ch 1, (puff st, dc) in top of turning ch; ch 3, turn.

Row 6: Puff st in first dc, ch 2, (puff st, ch 1, puff st) in next ch-1 sp; *ch 3, skip next ch-3 sp, (sc in next ch-3 sp, ch 3) twice, skip next ch-3 sp, (puff st, ch 1, puff st) in next ch-1 sp**, [ch 2, (puff st, ch 1, puff st) in next ch-1 sp] twice; rep from * across, ending last rep at **; ch 2, (puff st, dc) in top of turning ch; ch 3, turn.

Row 7: Puff st in first dc, picot, [(puff st, picot) twice] in next ch-2 sp, puff st in next ch-1 sp; *ch 3, skip next ch-3 sp, sc in next ch-3 sp, ch 3, skip next ch-3 sp, puff st in next ch-1 sp, picot; **[(puff st, picot) twice] in next ch-sp***; rep from ** twice; puff st in next ch-1 sp; rep from * across, ending last rep at ***; (puff st, dc) in top of turning ch. Finish off; weave in ends.

Clusters

STITCH GUIDE

Shell: Work (2 dc, ch 2, 2 dc) in specified st or sp: shell made.

Cl (cluster): (YO, insert hook in specified st or sp and draw up a lp, YO and draw through 2 lps on hook) 3 times, YO and draw through all 4 lps on hook: cl made.

Picot: Ch 3, sl st in 3rd ch from hook: picot made.

Instructions

Row 1 (wrong side): Ch 9, shell in 6th ch from hook, ch 2, skip next 2 chs, dc in last ch: 1 shell and 1 dc; ch 5, turn.

Row 2 (right side): Shell in ch-sp of shell, ch 1, dc in last dc of shell: 1 shell and 1 dc; ch 5, turn.

Row 3: Dc in first dc, ch 2, shell in ch-sp of shell, ch 2, skip next 2 chs, dc in next ch: 1 shell and 2 dc; ch 5, turn.

Row 4: Shell in ch-sp of shell, ch 1, dc in last dc of shell, ch 2, working along edge of rows, 10 dc in ch-5 sp at beg of previous row, sc in ch-5 sp at beg of row 2 rows before previous row: 1 shell, 11 dc and 1 sc; ch 2, turn.

Row 5: Skip first dc, sc in next dc, (ch 3, skip next dc, sc in next dc) 4 times, ch 2, skip next ch-2 sp, sc in next dc, ch 5, shell in ch-sp of shell, ch 2, skip next 2 chs, dc in next ch: 1 shell, 1 dc and 4 ch-3 sps; ch 5, turn.

Rep Rows 2 through 5 for desired length. At end of last row, do not ch 5.

Edging

Sl st in each st and ch across to ch-5 sp, sl st in first 2 chs of ch-5 sp, ch 1, sc in same ch-5 sp, ch 5; *skip next ch-2 sp, cl in next ch-3 sp, (ch 3, picot, ch 2, cl in next ch-3 sp) 3 times, skip next ch-2 sp; rep from * across; ch 5, sc in ch-5 sp at beg of Row 1. Finish off; weave in ends.

Fans

CHAIN MULTIPLE: 18 + 12

Instructions

Ch a multiple of 18 chs plus 12 additional chs.

Row 1 (right side): Dc in 6th ch from hook; *ch 1, skip next ch, dc in next ch; rep from * across; ch 1, turn.

Row 2: Skip first dc; *(sc in next ch-sp, sc in next dc) 3 times, sc in next ch-sp**, ch 3, skip next 2 ch-sps, 8 tr in next ch-sp, ch 3, skip next 2 ch-sps; rep from * across, ending last rep at **; ch 1, turn.

Row 3: Skip first sc, sc in next 5 sc; *ch 3, (dc in next tr, ch 1) 7 times, dc in next tr, ch 3, skip next sc, sc in next 5 sc; rep from * across; ch 1, turn.

Row 4: Skip first sc, sc in next 3 sc; *ch 5, skip next ch-3 sp, (sc in next ch-1 sp, ch 3) 6 times, sc in next ch-1 sp, ch 5, skip next sc, sc in next 3 sc; rep from * across; ch 1, turn.

Row 5: Skip first sc, sc in next sc; *ch 5, (tr in next ch-3 sp, ch 5, dc in top of last tr made) twice, (3 tr in next ch-3 sp, ch 5, dc in top of last tr made) twice, tr in next ch-3 sp, ch 5, dc in top of last tr made, tr in next ch-3 sp, ch 5, skip next sc, sc in next sc; rep from * across. Finish off; weave in ends.

Fans and Checks

CHAIN MULTIPLE: 20 + 2

STITCH GUIDE

Picot: Ch 3, sl st in top of last dc made before ch-3: picot made.

Instructions

Ch a multiple of 20 chs plus 2 additional chs.

Row 1 (right side): Sc in 2nd ch from hook and in each rem ch across; ch 3 (counts as dc on following row now and throughout), turn.

Row 2: Dc in first sc, ch 2, skip next 4 sc, 4 dc in next sc; *ch 3, skip next 4 sc, (tr, ch 2, tr) in next sc, ch 3, skip next 4 sc, 4 dc in next sc**, (ch 2, skip next 4 sc, 4 dc in next sc) twice; rep from * across, ending last rep at **; ch 2, skip next 4 sc, 2 dc in last sc; ch 4 (counts as dc and ch-1 sp on following row), turn.

Row 3: Work 4 dc in next ch-2 sp; *ch 3, skip next ch-3 sp, 9 tr in next ch-2 sp, ch 3, skip next ch-3 sp, 4 dc in next ch-2 sp**, ch 2, 4 dc in next ch-2 sp; rep from * across, ending last rep at **; ch 1, skip next dc, dc in top of turning ch; ch 3, turn.

Row 4: Dc in first dc; *ch 3, skip next ch-3 sp, skip next tr, dc in sp before next tr, (ch 1, dc in sp before next tr) 7 times, ch 3, skip next ch-3 sp**, 4 dc in next ch-2 sp; rep from * across, ending last rep at **; 2 dc in 3rd ch of turning ch-4; ch 1, turn.

Row 5: Sc in first dc, ch 1, 2 dc in next ch-3 sp, picot; *(2 dc in next ch-1 sp, picot) 7 times**, (2 dc in next ch-3 sp, picot) twice; rep from * across, ending last rep at **; 2 dc in last ch-3 sp, ch 1, skip next dc, sc in top of turning ch. Finish off; weave in ends.

Blades

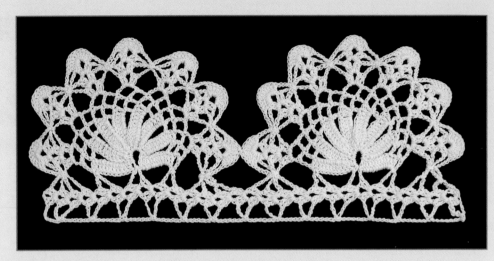

STITCH GUIDE

Shell: Work (2 dc, ch 2, 2 dc) in specified st or sp: shell made.

Instructions

Braid

Row 1 (wrong side): Ch 8, shell in 8th ch from hook: 1 shell; ch 7, turn.

Row 2 (right side): Shell in ch-sp of shell; ch 7, turn.

Rows 3 through 6: Rep Row 2, 4 more times.

Row 7: Shell in ch-sp of shell, ch 11, sl st in 10th ch from hook to form a ring, ch 7, sl st in ch-7 sp on edge of Braid on previous row: 1 shell, 1 ring and 1 ch-7 sp; ch 5, turn.

Blades

Row 1 (right side): Work 11 dc in ch-7 sp, sc in ring: 11 dc; ch 7, turn.

Row 2: Skip first 8 dc, dc in next dc, ch 2, skip next dc, dc in next dc, ch 2, skip next 2 chs, dc in next ch: 3 dc, 1 ch-7 sp and 2 ch-2 sps; ch 5, turn.

Row 3: Skip first dc, dc in next dc, ch 2, skip next ch-2 sp, dc in next dc, 10 dc in ch-7 sp, sc in ring: 12 dc and 1 ch-2 sp; ch 7, turn.

Row 4: Skip first 8 dc, dc in next dc, ch 2, skip next dc, dc in next dc, ch 2, skip next ch-2 sp, dc in next dc: 3 dc, 1 ch-7 sp and 2 ch-2 sps; ch 5, turn.

Rows 5 through 14: Rep Rows 3 and 4, 5 more times

Row 15: Rep Row 3. At end of row, ch 3 (instead of 7). Do NOT turn.

Braid (continued)

Row 8 (right side): Shell in ch-sp of shell: 1 shell; ch 7, turn.

Row 9: Shell in ch-sp of shell; ch 3, skip first 9 dc on Row 15 of Blades, sl st in next dc, ch 3, turn.

Row 10: Rep Row 8.

Braid and Blades

Row 11 (wrong side): Shell in ch-sp of shell; working around edge of Blade, ch 6, shell in ch-5 sp at beg of last row on Blades, (ch 6, skip next row on Blades, shell in ch-5 sp at beg of next row on Blades) 6 times: 8 shells and 7 ch-6 sps; ch 6, sl st in ch-7 sp on edge of Braid 2 rows before last sl st worked on Braid; ch 6, turn.

Row 12: (Shell in ch-sp of next shell, ch 7) 7 times; working on Braid, shell in ch-sp of shell: 8 shells and 7 ch-7 sps; ch 7, turn.

Row 13: Shell in ch-sp of shell; working around Blades, (ch 8, shell in ch-sp of next shell) 7 times: 8 shells and 7 ch-8 sps; ch 8, sl st in ch-7 sp on edge of Braid 2 rows before last sl st worked on Braid; ch 4, turn.

Row 14: Sc around 3 ch-sps (on last 3 rows) below, ch 4, (10 dc in ch-sp of next shell, ch 4, sc around 3 ch-sps below, ch 4) 7 times; working on Braid, shell in ch-sp of shell: 70 dc, 1 shell and 8 sc; ch 7, turn.

Braid (continued)

Row 15: Rep Row 2 on Braid.

Second and Subsequent Blades

Rep Rows 2 through 13 of Braid (including rows of Blades and rows of Braid and Blades).

Row 14: Sc around 3 ch-sps (on last 3 rows) below, ch 4, work 5 dc in ch-sp of first shell on current Blade, drop lp from hook, insert hook from front to back in 6th dc worked on last group of 10 dc on previous Blade, draw dropped lp through to front, work 5 more dc in ch-sp of same shell on current Blade, ch 4, sc around 3 ch-sps below, ch 4, (10 dc in ch-sp of next shell, ch 4, sc around 3 ch-sps below, ch 4) 6 times; working on Braid, shell in ch-sp of shell: 70 dc, 1 shell and 8 sc; ch 7, turn.

Braid (continued)

Row 15: Rep Row 2 on Braid.

Rep Rows 2 through 15 for desired length, ending last Blade by working a Row 14 rep. At end of last row, do NOT turn.

Straight Edge

Rotate piece to work on unworked edge of Braid. Sc in first ch-7 sp; *ch 6, sc in next ch-7 sp; rep from * across to beg of Braid. Finish off; weave in ends.

Filet and Scallops

STITCH GUIDE

Picot: Ch 4, sc in 4th ch from hook: picot made.

Instructions

Center Section

Row 1 (right side): Ch 20, dc in 8th ch from hook, (ch 1, skip next ch, dc in next ch) 6 times: 7 dc and 6 ch-1 sps; ch 5, turn.

Row 2: Dc in first dc, (dc in next ch-1 sp, dc in next dc) 6 times: 13 dc; ch 7, turn.

Row 3: Dc in first 5 dc, ch 5, skip next 5 dc, dc in next 3 dc, 2 dc in next ch-sp: 10 dc and 1 ch-5 sp; ch 7, turn.

Row 4: Dc in 6th and 7th chs from hook, dc in next 3 dc, ch 4, (sc, ch 3, sc) in next ch-5 sp, ch 4, skip next 2 dc, dc in next 3 dc: 8 dc, 2 sc and 3 ch-sps; ch 7, turn.

Row 5: Dc in first 3 dc, 2 dc in next ch-4 sp, ch 5, skip next ch-3 sp, 2 dc in next ch-4 sp, dc in next 3 dc, leave last 2 dc unworked: 10 dc and 1 ch-5 sp; ch 4, turn.

Row 6: Skip first 2 dc, dc in next 3 dc, 5 dc in next ch-5 sp, dc in next 5 dc: 13 dc; ch 7, turn.

Row 7: Dc in first dc, (ch 1, skip next dc, dc in next dc) 6 times: 7 dc and 6 ch-1 sps; ch 5, turn.

Rep Rows 2 through 7 for desired length. At end of last row, do not ch 5 and do not turn.

Scalloped Edging

Row 1 (right side): Rotate piece to work along edge of rows, ch 1, sc in top of last dc worked; *ch 4, (sc, ch 4, sc) in next turning ch-sp, ch 4, (sc, ch 4, sc, ch 7, sc, ch 4, sc) in next turning ch-sp, ch 4, (sc, ch 4, sc) in next turning ch-sp; rep from * across; ch 4, sc in ch at base of last dc on Row 1; ch 6, turn.

Row 2: Skip first 2 ch-4 sps, tr in next ch-4 sp; *ch 2, skip next ch-4 sp, [(tr, ch 2) 5 times, tr] in next ch-7 sp**, (ch 2, skip next ch-4 sp, tr in next ch-4 sp) 3 times; rep from * across, ending last rep at **; ch 2, skip next ch-4 sp, tr in next ch-4 sp, ch 2, skip last 2 ch-4 sps, tr in last sc; ch 1, turn.

Row 3: *Work 3 sc in each of next 2 ch-2 sps, (2 sc, picot, 2 sc) in each of next 5 ch-2 sps, 3 sc in each of next 2 ch-2 sps; rep from * across, working last 3 sc in turning ch-6 sp, sl st in 4th ch of turning ch-6 sp. Finish off; weave in ends.

Straight Edging

Row 1 (wrong side): With wrong side facing, join with sl st in turning ch-sp at beg of last row on Center Section, ch 1, (sc, ch 4, sc) in same ch-sp as joining; *ch 4, (sc, ch 4, sc) in next turning ch-sp; rep from * across; ch 7, turn.

Row 2: Skip first ch-4 sp, dc in next ch-4 sp; *ch 5, skip next ch-4 sp, dc in next ch-4 sp; rep from * across to last ch-4 sp; ch 3, skip last ch-4 sp, tr in last sc; ch 1, turn.

Row 3: Sc in first tr, 3 sc in next ch-3 sp, sc in next dc; *5 sc in next ch-5 sp, sc in next dc; rep from * across to turning ch-7 sp; 3 sc in turning ch-7 sp, sc in 4th ch of turning ch-7; ch 4, turn.

Row 4: Skip first 2 sc, dc in next sc; *ch 1, skip next sc, dc in next sc; rep from * across. Finish off; weave in ends.

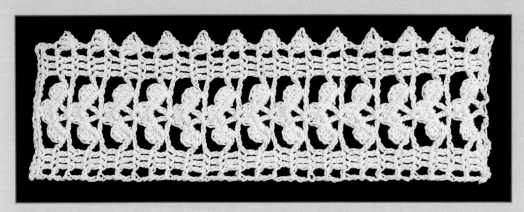

Triple Shells

STITCH GUIDE

Shell: Work (sc, ch 1, 3 dc, sc) in specified st or sp: shell made.

Instructions

Row 1 (wrong side): Ch 22, sc in 2nd ch from hook, ch 1, skip next ch, sc in next 3 chs, ch 2, skip next 2 chs, sc in next ch, ch 2, skip next 2 chs, (dc, ch 2, dc) in next ch, (ch 2, skip next 2 chs, sc in next ch) twice, sc in next 2 chs, ch 1, skip next ch, sc in last ch: 2 dc, 10 sc, 5 ch-2 sps and 2 ch-1 sps; ch 3, turn.

Row 2 (right side): Work 3 dc in first sc, ch 1, dc in next 3 sc, ch 2, skip next ch-2 sp, shell in each of next 3 ch-2 sps, ch 2, skip next ch-2 sp, dc in next 3 sc, ch 1, dc in last sc: 3 shells, 10 dc, 2 ch-2 sps and 2 ch-1 sps; ch 4 (counts as dc and ch-1 sp on following row now and throughout), turn.

Row 3: Skip first dc, dc in next 3 dc, ch 2, skip next shell, [(dc, ch 2) 3 times, dc] in center dc of next shell, ch 2, skip next shell, dc in next 3 dc, ch 1, dc in next dc, leave rem dc unworked: 12 dc, 5 ch-2 sps and 2 ch-1 sps; ch 3, turn.

Row 4: Work 3 dc in first dc, ch 1, dc in next 3 dc, ch 2, skip next ch-2 sp, shell in each of next 3 ch-2 sps, ch 2, skip next ch-2 sp, dc in next 3 dc, ch 1, skip next ch, dc in next ch: 3 shells, 10 dc, 2 ch-2 sps and 2 ch-1 sps; ch 4, turn.

Rep Rows 3 and 4 for desired length.

Next Row (wrong side): Skip first dc, dc in next 3 dc, ch 5, skip next shell, sc in center dc of next shell, ch 5, skip next shell, dc in next 3 dc, ch 1, dc in next dc, leave rem dc unworked: 8 dc, 1 sc, 2 ch-5 sps and 2 ch-1 sps; ch 1, turn.

Last Row (right side): Sc in first dc, ch 1, sc in next 3 dc; *ch 2, skip next 2 chs, sc in next ch, ch 2, skip next 2 chs**, sc in next sc; rep from * to ** once; sc in next 3 dc, ch 1, skip next ch, sc in next ch: 11 sc, 4 ch-2 sps and 2 ch-1 sps. Finish off; weave in ends.

Triple Clusters

STITCH GUIDE

3-tr cl (3 triple crochet cluster): *YO twice, insert hook in specified ch-sp and draw up a lp, (YO and draw through 2 lps on hook) twice; rep from * 2 more times in same ch-sp; YO and draw through all 4 lps on hook: 3-tr cl made.

Beg 3-tr cl (beginning 3 triple crochet cluster): Ch 4; *YO twice, insert hook in specified ch-sp and draw up a lp, (YO and draw through 2 lps on hook) twice; rep from * once more in same ch-sp; YO and draw through all 3 lps on hook: beg 3-tr cl made.

Instructions

Row 1 (wrong side): Ch 14, sc in 9th ch from hook, ch 5, skip next 4 chs, sc in last ch: 2 sc and 2 ch-sps; turn.

Row 2 (right side): Work beg 3-tr cl in first ch-sp, (ch 3, 3-tr cl in same ch-sp) twice, ch 5, [(3-tr cl, ch 3) twice, 3-tr cl] in next ch-sp: six 3-tr cl and 5 ch-sps; ch 5, turn.

Row 3: Sc in first ch-sp, (ch 5, sc in next ch-sp) 3 times, leave rem ch-sp unworked: 4 sc and 4 ch-sps; turn.

Row 4: Work beg 3-tr cl in first ch-sp, (ch 3, 3-tr cl in same ch-sp) twice, ch 5, [(3-tr cl, ch 3) twice, 3-tr cl] in next ch-sp, leave 2 rem ch-sps unworked: six 3-tr cl and 5 ch-sps; ch 5, turn.

Rep Rows 3 and 4 for desired length.

Last Row: Sc in first ch-sp, (ch 5, sc in next ch-sp) 3 times, ch 6, sc in last ch-sp: 5 sc and 5 ch-sps; do NOT turn.

Straight Edge

Row 1 (wrong side): *Ch 6, skip next row, sc in unworked ch-sp at edge of next row; rep from * across; ch 3, dc in foundation ch at base of last sc worked on Row 1; ch 1, turn.

Row 2: Sc in dc, 3 sc in ch-3 sp, sc in next sc; *6 sc in next ch-6 sp, sc in next sc; rep from * across to ch-6 sp worked at end of Last Row; 3 sc in last ch-6 sp, sc in 3rd ch of same ch-6 sp. Finish off; weave in ends.

Spider Webs

STITCH GUIDE

Picot: Ch 3, sc in 3rd ch from hook: picot made.

Instructions

Ch 29.

Row 1 (right side): Dc in 8th ch from hook (skipped chs count as dc and ch-2 sp), ch 2, skip next 2 chs, dc in next 4 chs, ch 5, skip next 3 chs, sc in next 5 chs, ch 5, skip next 3 chs, dc in last 4 chs: 2 ch-5 sps and 2 ch-2 sps; ch 7, turn.

Row 2: Work 4 dc in first dc, ch 3, skip next 2 dc, dc in next dc, 3 dc in next ch-5 sp, ch 5, skip next sc, sc in next 3 sc, ch 5, 3 dc in next ch-5 sp, dc in next dc, ch 2, skip next 2 dc, (dc in next dc, ch 2) twice, skip next 2 chs, dc in next ch: 2 ch-5 sps, 1 ch-3 sp and 3 ch-2 sps; ch 5 (counts as dc and ch-2 sp on following row), turn.

Row 3: Skip first ch-2 sp, (dc in next dc, ch 2) 3 times, skip next 2 dc, dc in next dc, 3 dc in next ch-5 sp, ch 5, skip next sc, sc in next sc, ch 5, 3 dc in next ch-5 sp, dc in next dc, ch 5, sc in next ch-3 sp, ch 5, skip next 3 dc, dc in next dc, 3 dc in turning ch-7 sp: 4 ch-5 sps and 4 ch-2 sps; ch 7, turn.

Row 4: Work 4 dc in first dc, ch 5, sc in next ch-5 sp, sc in next sc, sc in next ch-5 sp, ch 5, skip next 3 dc, dc in next dc, 3 dc in next ch-5 sp, ch 2, 3 dc in next ch-5 sp, dc in next dc, ch 2, skip next 2 dc, (dc in next dc, ch 2) 4 times, skip next 2 chs, dc in next ch: 2 ch-5 sps and 6 ch-2 sps; ch 5 (counts as dc and ch-2 sp on following row), turn.

Row 5: Skip first ch-2 sp, (dc in next dc, ch 2) 5 times, skip next 2 dc, dc in next dc, 2 dc in next ch-2 sp, dc in next dc, ch 5, sc in next ch-5 sp, sc in next 3 sc, sc in next ch-5 sp, ch 5, skip next 3 dc, dc in next dc, 3 dc in turning ch-7 sp: 2 ch-5 sps and 6 ch-2 sps; ch 7, turn.

Row 6: Work 4 dc in first dc, ch 3, skip next 2 dc, dc in next dc, 3 dc in next ch-5 sp, ch 5, skip next sc, sc in next 3 sc, ch 5, 3 dc in next ch-5 sp, dc in next dc, ch 3, skip next 2 dc, dc in next dc, 2 dc in next ch-2 sp, (dc in next dc, ch 2) 5 times, skip next 2 chs, dc in next ch: 2 ch-5 sps, 2 ch-3 sps and 5 ch-2 sps; ch 5 (counts as dc and ch-2 sp on following row), turn.

Row 7: Skip first ch-2 sp, (dc in next dc, ch 2) 3 times, dc in next dc, 2 dc in next ch-2 sp; *dc in next dc, ch 5, sc in next ch-3 sp, ch 5, skip next 3 dc, dc in next dc**, 3 dc in next ch-5 sp, ch 5, skip next sc, sc in next sc, ch 5, 3 dc in next ch-5 sp; rep from * to ** once; 3 dc in turning ch-7 sp: 6 ch-5 sps and 4 ch-2 sps; ch 7, turn.

Row 8: Work 4 dc in first dc; *ch 5, sc in next ch-5 sp, sc in next sc, sc in next ch-5 sp, ch 5, skip next 3 dc, dc in next dc**, 3 dc in next ch-5 sp, ch 2, 3 dc in next ch-5 sp, dc in next dc; rep from * to ** once; 2 dc in next ch-2 sp, (dc in next dc, ch 2) 3 times, skip next 2 chs, dc in next ch: 4 ch-5 sps, and 4 ch-2 sps; ch 5 (counts as dc and ch-2 sp on following row), turn.

Row 9: Skip first ch-2 sp, dc in next dc, ch 2; *dc in next dc, 2 dc in next ch-2 sp, dc in next dc, ch 5, sc in next ch-5 sp, sc in next 3 sc, sc in next ch-5 sp, ch 5, skip next 3 dc; rep from * once; dc in next dc, 3 dc in turning ch-7 sp: 4 ch-5 sps and 2 ch-2 sps; ch 5, turn.

Row 10: Skip first 3 dc; *dc in next dc, 3 dc in next ch-5 sp, ch 5, skip next sc, sc in next 3 sc, ch 5, 3 dc in next ch-5 sp, dc in next dc**, ch 3, skip next 2 dc; rep from * to ** once; ch 2, skip next 2 dc, (dc in next dc, ch 2) twice, skip next 2 chs, dc in next ch: 4 ch-5 sps, 1 ch-3 sp and 3 ch-2 sps; ch 5 (counts as dc and ch-2 sp on following row), turn.

Row 11: Skip first ch-2 sp, (dc in next dc, ch 2) 3 times, skip next 2 dc; *dc in next dc, 3 dc in next ch-5 sp, ch 5, skip next sc, sc in next sc, ch 5, 3 dc in next ch-5 sp, dc in next dc**, ch 5, sc in next ch-3 sp, ch 5, skip next 3 dc; rep from * to ** once: 6 ch-5 sps and 4 ch-2 sps; ch 5, turn.

Row 12: Skip first 3 dc; *dc in next dc, 3 dc in next ch-5 sp, ch 2, 3 dc in next ch-5 sp, dc in next dc**, ch 5, sc in next ch-5 sp, sc in next sc, sc in next ch-5 sp, ch 5, skip next 3 dc; rep from * to ** once; ch 2, skip next 2 dc, (dc in next dc, ch 2) 4 times, skip next 2 chs, dc in next ch: 2 ch-5 sps and 7 ch-2 sps; ch 5 (counts as dc and ch-2 sp on following row), turn.

Row 13: Skip first ch-2 sp, (dc in next dc, ch 2) 5 times, skip next 2 dc, dc in next dc, 2 dc in next ch-2 sp, dc in next dc, ch 5, sc in next ch-5 sp, sc in next 3 sc, sc in next ch-5 sp, ch 5, skip next 3 dc, dc in next dc, 2 dc in next ch-2 sp, dc in next dc: 2 ch-5 sps and 6 ch-2 sps; ch 5, turn.

Row 14: Skip first 3 dc, dc in next dc, 3 dc in next ch-5 sp, ch 5, skip next sc, sc in next 3 sc, ch 5, 3 dc in next ch-5 sp, dc in next dc, ch 3, skip next 2 dc, dc in next dc, 2 dc in next ch-2 sp, (dc in next dc, ch 2) 5 times, skip next 2 chs, dc in next ch: 2 ch-5 sps, 1 ch-3 sp and 5 ch-2 sps; ch 5 (counts as dc and ch-2 sp on following row), turn.

Row 15: Skip first ch-2 sp, (dc in next dc, ch 2) 3 times, dc in next dc, 2 dc in next ch-2 sp, dc in next dc, ch 5, sc in next ch-3 sp, ch 5, skip next 3 dc, dc in next dc, 3 dc in next ch-5 sp, ch 5, skip next sc, sc in next sc, ch 5, 3 dc in next ch-5 sp, dc in next dc: 4 ch-5 sps and 4 ch-2 sps; ch 5, turn.

Row 16: Skip first 3 dc, dc in next dc, 3 dc in next ch-5 sp, ch 2, 3 dc in next ch-5 sp, dc in next dc, ch 5, sc in next ch-5 sp, sc in next sc, sc in next ch-5 sp, ch 5, skip next 3 dc, dc in next dc, 2 dc in next ch-2 sp, (dc in next dc, ch 2) 3 times, skip next 2 chs, dc in next ch: 2 ch-5 sps and 4 ch-2 sps; ch 5 (counts as dc and ch-2 sp on following row), turn.

Row 17: Skip first ch-2 sp, dc in next dc, ch 2, dc in next dc, 2 dc in next ch-2 sp, dc in next dc, ch 5, sc in next ch-5 sp, sc in next 3 sc, sc in next ch-5 sp, ch 5, skip next 3 dc, dc in next dc, 2 dc in next ch-2 sp, dc in next dc: 2 ch-5 sps and 2 ch-2 sps; ch 7, turn.

Rep Rows 2 through 17 for desired length. At end of last row, ch 5 instead of ch 7. Do NOT turn or finish off. Rotate piece to work along edge of rows.

Edge

Work (dc, ch 1, picot, ch 1, dc) in next ch-sp; *ch 1, picot, ch 1, (dc, ch 1, picot, ch 1, dc) in next ch-sp; rep from * across; ch 5, sl st in ch at base of last dc on Row 1. Finish off; weave in ends.

Scallops and X's

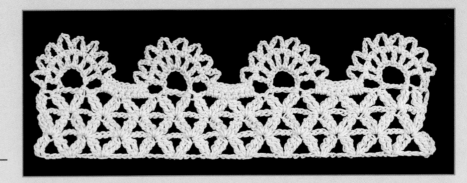

CHAIN MULTIPLE: 15

STITCH GUIDE

Cl (cluster): *YO twice, insert hook in specified st or sp and draw up a lp, (YO and draw through 2 lps on hook) twice; rep from * once more in same st or sp; YO and draw through all 3 lps on hook: cl made.

Instructions

Ch a multiple of 15 chs.

Row 1 (right side): Cl in 5th ch from hook; *skip next 4 chs, (cl, ch 4, cl) in next ch; rep from * across to last 5 chs; skip next 4 chs, cl in last ch; ch 4, turn.

Row 2: (Cl, ch 4, cl) in first cl; *skip next cl and next ch-4 sp, (cl, ch 4, cl) in next cl; rep from * across; ch 4, turn.

Row 3: Cl in first cl, skip next ch-4 sp; *cl in next cl, ch 10, tr in top of last cl made, cl in same cl as last cl made, skip next cl and next ch-4 sp**, [(cl, ch 4, cl) in next cl, skip next cl and next ch-4 sp] twice; rep from * across, ending last rep at **; cl in last cl; ch 2, turn.

Row 4: *Skip first ch of next ch-10 sp, dc in next ch, (ch 1, dc in next ch) 7 times, ch 2**, 3 sc in next ch-4 sp, sc in next 2 cl, 3 sc in next ch-4 sp, ch 2; rep from * across, ending last rep at **; sc in last cl; ch 1, turn.

Row 5: *Sc in next ch-2 sp, (ch 5, sc in next ch-1 sp) 7 times, ch 5, sc in next ch-2 sp**, skip next sc, sc in next 6 sc, skip next sc; rep from * across, ending last rep at **. Finish off; weave in ends.

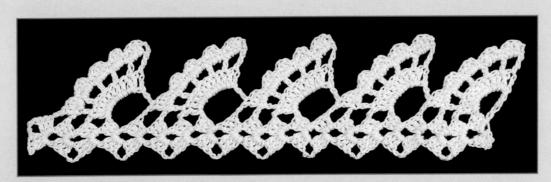

Fans and Shells

STITCH GUIDE

Shell: Work (3 dc, ch 3, 3 dc) in specified st or sp: shell made.

Instructions

Row 1 (wrong side): Ch 7, shell in 4th ch from hook, ch 7, skip next 2 chs, dc in last ch: 1 shell, 1 dc and 1 ch-7 sp; ch 3, turn.

Row 2 (right side): Work 10 dc in ch-7 sp, ch 2, shell in ch-sp of shell: 1 shell, 10 dc and 1 ch-2 sp; ch 3, turn.

Row 3: Shell in ch-sp of shell, ch 2, skip next ch-2 sp, dc in next dc, (ch 2, skip next dc, dc in next dc) 4 times, ch 2, skip last dc, dc in 3rd ch of turning ch-3: 1 shell, 6 dc and 6 ch-2 sps; ch 3, turn.

Row 4: Work (3 dc, sc) in first ch-2 sp, [(sc, 3 dc, sc) in next ch-2 sp] 3 times, (sc, 2 dc) in next ch-2 sp, dc in next dc, ch 2, shell in ch-sp of shell: 1 shell, 15 dc, 8 sc and 1 ch-2 sp; ch 3, turn.

Row 5: Shell in ch-sp of shell, ch 7, skip next ch-2 sp, dc in next dc: 1 shell, 1 dc and 1 ch-7 sp; ch 3, turn.

Rep Rows 2 through 5 for desired length, ending by working a Row 4 rep. At end of last row, do NOT ch 3. Finish off; weave in ends.

Shamrocks

STITCH GUIDE

Shamrock Leaf: Work (sc, hdc, dc, tr, dc, hdc, sc) in specified ch-sp: shamrock leaf made.

Instructions

Ch 21.

Row 1 (wrong side): Dc in 8th ch from hook (skipped chs count as dc and ch-2 sp), (ch 2, skip next 2 chs, dc in next ch) 3 times, ch 5, skip next 3 chs, [(dc, ch 3) 3 times, dc] in last ch: 4 ch-2 sps, 1 ch-5 sp and 3 ch-3 sps; turn.

Row 2 (right side): Work shamrock leaf in each of next 3 ch-3 sps, ch 5, dc in next ch-5 sp, (ch 2, dc in next dc) 4 times, ch 2, skip next 2 chs, dc in next ch: 3 shamrock leaves, 1 ch-5 sp and 5 ch-2 sps; ch 5 (counts as dc and ch-2 sp on following row), turn.

Row 3: Skip first 2 chs, (dc in next dc, ch 2) 5 times, dc in next ch-5 sp, ch 7, in tr of center shamrock leaf work [(dc, ch 3) 3 times, dc]: 6 ch-2 sps, 1 ch-7 sp and 3 ch-3 sps; turn.

Row 4: Work shamrock leaf in each of next 3 ch-3 sps, ch 5, dc in next ch-7 sp, (ch 2, dc in next dc) 6 times, ch 2, skip next 2 chs, dc in next ch: 3 shamrock leaves, 1 ch-5 sp and 7 ch-2 sps; ch 5 (counts as dc and ch-2 sp on following row), turn.

Row 5: Skip first 2 chs, (dc in next dc, ch 2) 7 times, dc in next ch-5 sp, ch 7, in tr of center shamrock leaf work [(dc, ch 3) 3 times, dc]: 8 ch-2 sps, 1 ch-7 sp and 3 ch-3 sps; turn.

Row 6: Work shamrock leaf in each of next 3 ch-3 sps, ch 5, dc in next ch-7 sp, (ch 2, dc in next dc) 8 times, ch 2, skip next 2 chs, dc in next ch: 3 shamrock leaves, 1 ch-5 sp and 9 ch-2 sps; ch 5 (counts as dc and ch-2 sp on following row), turn.

Row 7: Skip first 2 chs, dc in next dc, (ch 2, dc in next dc) 3 times, ch 7, skip next 4 ch-2 sps, in next ch-2 sp work [(dc, ch 3) 3 times, dc]: 4 ch-2 sps, 1 ch-7 sp and 3 ch-3 sps; turn.

Row 8: Work shamrock leaf in each of next 3 ch-3 sps, ch 5, dc in next ch-7 sp, (ch 2, dc in next dc) 4 times, ch 2, skip next 2 chs, dc in next ch: 3 shamrock leaves, 1 ch-5 sp and 5 ch-2 sps; ch 5 (counts as dc and ch-2 sp on following row), turn.

Rep Rows 3 through 8 for desired length, ending with a Row 6 rep. Finish off; weave in ends.

Curved Peaks

STITCH GUIDE

Shell: Work (3 dc, ch 2, 3 dc) in specified st or sp: shell made.

Picot: Ch 5, sc in top of last hdc made before ch-5: picot made.

Instructions

Row 1 (right side): Ch 5, shell in 5th ch from hook: 1 shell; ch 3, turn.

Row 2: Shell in ch-sp of shell, ch 8, sc in turning ch-sp of previous shell: 1 shell and 1 ch-8 sp; ch 1, turn.

Row 3: Work 12 hdc in ch-8 sp, ch 1, shell in ch-sp to form bottom edge shown in photo: 1 shell and 12 hdc; ch 3, turn.

Row 4: Shell in ch-sp of shell, ch 8, then rotating piece to work along upper edge, sc in ch-1 sp: 1 shell and 1 ch-8 sp; ch 1, turn.

Row 5: Work 6 hdc in ch-8 sp, ch 8, turn; continuing on side edge, skip next 12 hdc, sc in sp before next hdc, ch 1, turn; 12 hdc in ch-8 sp, 6 hdc in rem part of ch-8 sp to complete loop; now continue on shell strip, working ch 1, shell in ch-sp of shell, tr in turning ch-sp: 1 shell, 1 tr and 24 hdc; ch 3, turn.

Row 6: Shell in ch-sp of shell, ch 8, working in upper section sc in next ch-1 sp: 1 shell and 1 ch-8 sp; ch 1, turn.

Row 7: (Work 6 hdc in ch-8 sp, ch 8, turn; skip next 12 hdc, sc in sp before next hdc, ch 1, turn) twice; (6 hdc, picot, 6 hdc) in ch-8 sp, (6 hdc in rem ch-8 sp) twice, ch 1, shell in ch-sp of shell, tr in turning ch-sp: 1 shell, 1 tr, 36 hdc and 1 picot; ch 3, turn.

Row 8: Shell in ch-sp of shell, ch 8, sc in ch-1 sp: 1 shell and 1 ch-8 sp; ch 1, turn.

Rep Rows 3 through 8 for desired length, ending by working a Row 7 rep. At end of last row, do NOT ch 1. Finish off; weave in ends.

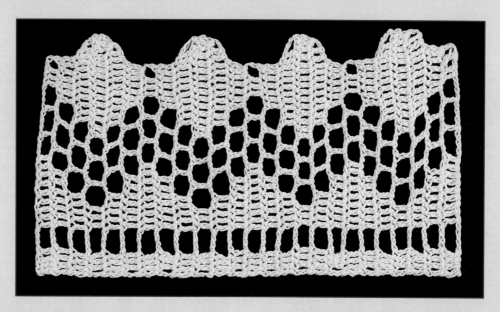

Filet Zigzags

Instructions

Ch 33.

Row 1 (right side): Dc in 4th ch from hook (skipped chs count as first dc), dc in next 2 chs, (ch 3, skip next 3 chs, dc in next ch) 3 times, dc in next 8 chs, ch 3, skip next 3 chs, dc in last 4 chs: 19 dc and 4 ch-3 sps; ch 3 (counts as dc on following row now and throughout), turn.

Row 2: Skip first dc, dc in next 3 dc, ch 3, skip next ch-3 sp, dc in next 7 dc, ch 3, skip next 2 dc, dc in center ch of next ch-3 sp, (ch 3, skip next dc, dc in center ch of next ch-3 sp) twice, dc in next ch, dc in next 3 dc, 2 dc in turning ch-sp: 20 dc and 4 ch-3 sps; ch 5 (counts as dc and 2 chs on following row), turn.

Row 3: Dc in 4th and 5th chs from hook, dc in next 7 dc, dc in next 2 chs, (ch 3, skip next dc, dc in center ch of next ch-3 sp) twice, ch 3, skip next 2 dc, dc in next 5 dc, ch 3, skip next ch-3 sp, dc in next 3 dc, dc in top of turning ch: 23 dc and 4 ch-3 sps; ch 3, turn.

Row 4: Skip first dc, dc in next 3 dc, ch 3, skip next ch-3 sp, dc in next 3 dc, ch 3, skip next 2 dc, dc in center ch of next ch-3 sp, (ch 3, skip next dc, dc in center ch of next ch-3 sp) twice, dc in next ch, dc in next 11 dc, 2 dc in turning ch-sp: 24 dc and 4 ch-3 sps; ch 3, turn.

Row 5: Skip first 2 dc, dc in next 11 dc, ch 3, skip next 2 dc, dc in center ch of next ch-3 sp, (ch 3, skip next dc, dc in center ch of next ch-3 sp) twice, dc in next ch, dc in next 3 dc, ch 3, skip next ch-3 sp, dc in next 3 dc, dc in top of turning ch: 23 dc and 4 ch-3 sps; ch 3, turn.

Row 6: Skip first dc, dc in next 3 dc, ch 3, skip next ch-3 sp, dc in next 5 dc, dc in next 2 chs, (ch 3, skip next dc, dc in center ch of next ch-3 sp) twice, ch 3, skip next 2 dc, dc in next 7 dc: 20 dc and 4 ch-3 sps; ch 3, turn.

Row 7: Skip first 2 dc, dc in next 3 dc, ch 3, skip next 2 dc, dc in center ch of next ch-3 sp, (ch 3, skip next dc, dc in center ch of next ch-3 sp) twice, dc in next ch, dc in next 7 dc, ch 3, skip next ch-3 sp, dc in next 3 dc, dc in top of turning ch: 19 dc and 4 ch-3 sps; ch 3, turn.

Rep Rows 2 through 7 for desired length. Finish off; weave in ends.

Diamonds & Swirls

Instructions

Ch 52.

Row 1 (wrong side): Dc in 8th ch from hook (skipped chs count as dc and ch-2 sp), (ch 2, skip next 2 chs, dc in next ch) twice, dc in next 3 chs, ch 5, skip next 4 chs, dc in next 16 chs, ch 5, skip next 4 chs, dc in next 4 chs, ch 8, skip next 6 chs, sl st in last ch: 27 dc, 1 ch-8 sp, 2 ch-5 sps and 3 ch-2 sps; ch 1, turn.

Row 2 (right side): Work 18 dc in ch-8 sp, skip next 3 dc, dc in next dc, dc in next 3 chs, ch 5, skip next 3 dc, dc in next 10 dc, ch 5, skip next 3 chs, dc in next 2 chs, dc in next 4 dc, (ch 2, skip next ch-2 sp, dc in next dc) twice, ch 2, skip next 2 chs, dc in next ch: 41 dc, 2 ch-5 sps and 3 ch-2 sps; ch 5 (counts as dc and ch-2 sp on following row now and throughout), turn.

Row 3: Skip first dc, dc in next dc, (ch 2, skip next ch-2 sp, dc in next dc) twice, dc in next 5 dc, dc in next 2 chs, ch 5, skip next 3 dc, dc in next 4 dc, ch 5, skip next 2 chs, dc in next 3 chs, dc in next dc, ch 4, skip next 6 dc, dc in next 4 dc, ch 8, skip next 3 dc, sl st in next dc: 23 dc, 1 ch-8 sp, 2 ch-5 sps, 1 ch-4 sp and 3 ch-2 sps; ch 1, turn.

Row 4: Work 18 dc in ch-8 sp, (ch 4, skip next 3 dc, dc in next dc, dc in next 3 chs) twice, ch 9, skip next 4 dc, skip next 2 chs, dc in next 3 chs, dc in next dc, ch 4, skip next 3 dc, dc in next 4 dc, (ch 2, skip next ch-2 sp, dc in next dc) twice, ch 2, skip next 2 chs, dc in next ch: 37 dc, 1 ch-9 sp, 3 ch-4 sps and 3 ch-2 sps; ch 5, turn.

Row 5: Skip first dc, dc in next dc, (ch 2, skip next ch-2 sp, dc in next dc) twice, ch 2, skip next 2 dc, dc in next dc, dc in next 3 chs, ch 5, skip next 3 dc, dc in next dc, dc in next 9 chs, ch 5, skip next ch, dc in next 3 chs, dc in next dc, ch 2, skip next 2 dc, dc in next dc, dc in next 3 chs, ch 4, skip next 3 dc, dc in next 4 dc, ch 8, skip next 3 dc, sl st in next dc: 30 dc, 1 ch-8 sp, 2 ch-5 sps, 1 ch-4 sp and 5 ch-2 sps; ch 1, turn.

Row 6: Work 18 dc in ch-8 sp, ch 4, skip next ch, dc in next 3 chs, dc in next dc, ch 2, skip next 2 dc, dc in next dc, ch 2, skip next ch-2 sp, dc in next dc, ch 2, skip next 2 dc, dc in next dc, dc in next 3 chs, ch 5, skip next 3 dc, dc in next 4 dc, ch 5, skip next 2 chs, dc in next 3 chs, dc in next dc, ch 2, skip next 2 dc, dc in next dc, (ch 2, skip next ch-2 sp, dc in next dc) 3 times, ch 2, skip next 2 chs, dc in next ch: 41 dc, 2 ch-5 sps, 1 ch-4 sp and 8 ch-2 sps; ch 5, turn.

Row 7: Skip first dc, dc in next dc, (ch 2, skip next ch-2 sp, dc in next dc) 4 times, ch 2, skip next 2 dc, dc in next dc, dc in next 3 chs, ch 9, skip next 4 dc, skip next 2 chs, dc in next 3 chs, dc in next dc, ch 2, skip next 2 dc, dc in next dc, (ch 2, skip next ch-2 sp, dc in next dc) 3 times, ch 2, skip next 2 dc, dc in next dc, dc in next 3 chs, ch 4, skip next dc, dc in next 4 dc, ch 8, skip next 3 dc, sl st in next dc: 26 dc, 1 ch-9 sp, 1 ch-8 sp, 1 ch-4 sp and 11 ch-2 sps; ch 1, turn.

Row 8: Work 18 dc in ch-8 sp, ch 4, skip next ch, dc in next 3 chs, dc in next dc, ch 2, skip next 2 dc, dc in next dc, (ch 2, skip next ch-2 sp, dc in next dc) twice, dc in next 2 chs, dc in next dc, (ch 2, skip next ch-2 sp, dc in next dc) twice, ch 2, skip next 2 dc, dc in next dc, dc in next 9 chs, ch 2, skip next 3 dc, dc in next dc, (ch 2, skip next ch-2 sp, dc in next dc) 5 times, ch 2, skip next 2 chs, dc in next dc: 47 dc, 1 ch-4 sp and 13 ch-2 sps; ch 5, turn.

Row 9: Skip first dc, dc in next dc, (ch 2, skip next ch-2 sp, dc in next dc) 5 times, dc in next 2 chs, dc in next dc, ch 8, skip next 8 dc, dc in next dc, dc in next 2 chs, dc in next dc, (ch 2, skip next ch-2 sp, dc in next dc) twice, ch 2, skip next 2 dc, dc in next dc, (ch 2, skip next ch-2 sp, dc in next dc) twice, dc in next 2 chs, dc in next dc, ch 4, skip next 2 dc, dc in next dc, dc in next 3 chs, ch 8, skip next 6 dc, sl st in next dc: 26 dc, 2 ch-8 sps, 1 ch-4 sp and 11 ch-2 sps; ch 1, turn.

Row 10: Work 18 dc in ch-8 sp, dc in next 4 dc, dc in next 3 chs, ch 5, skip next 3 dc, dc in next dc, dc in next 2 chs, dc in next dc, (ch 2, skip next ch-2 sp, dc in next dc) 3 times, dc in next 2 chs, dc in next dc, ch 5, skip next 2 chs, dc in next 4 chs, ch 5, skip next 3 dc, dc in next dc, dc in next 2 chs, dc in next dc, (ch 2, skip next ch-2 sp, dc in next dc) 4 times, ch 2, skip next 2 chs, dc in next ch: 48 dc, 3 ch-5 sps and 8 ch-2 sps; ch 5, turn.

Row 11: Skip first dc, dc in next dc, (ch 2, skip next ch-2 sp, dc in next dc) 3 times, dc in next 2 chs, dc in next dc, ch 5, skip next 2 chs, dc in next 3 chs, dc in next 4 dc, dc in next 3 chs, ch 5, skip next 3 dc, dc in next dc, dc in next 2 chs, dc in next dc, ch 2, skip next ch-2 sp, dc in next dc, dc in next 2 chs, dc in next dc, ch 5, skip next 2 chs, dc in next 3 chs, dc in next dc, ch 8, skip next 7 dc, sl st in next dc: 30 dc, 1 ch-8 sp, 3 ch-5 sps and 5 ch-2 sps; ch 1, turn.

Row 12: Work 18 dc in ch-8 sp, dc in next 4 dc, dc in next 3 chs, ch 4, skip next 3 dc, dc in next dc, dc in next 2 chs, dc in next dc, ch 5, skip next 2 chs, dc in next 3 chs, dc in next dc, ch 8, skip next 8 dc, dc in next dc, dc in next 3 chs, ch 4, skip next 3 dc, dc in next dc, dc in next 2 chs, dc in next dc, (ch 2, skip next ch-2 sp, dc in next dc) twice, ch 2, skip next 2 chs, dc in next ch: 44 dc, 1 ch-8 sp, 1 ch-5 sp, 2 ch-4 sps and 3 ch-2 sps; ch 5, turn.

Row 13: Skip first dc, dc in next dc, (ch 2, skip next ch-2 sp, dc in next dc) twice, dc in next 3 dc, dc in next 4 chs, ch 5, skip next 2 chs, dc in next 4 chs, ch 5, skip next 3 dc, dc in next dc, dc in next 3 chs, ch 5, skip next 4 dc, skip next ch, dc in next 3 chs, dc in next dc, ch 8, skip next 6 dc, sl st in next dc: 23 dc, 1 ch-8 sp, 3 ch-5 sps and 3 ch-2 sps; ch 1, turn.

Row 14: Work 18 dc in ch-8 sp, dc in next 4 dc, dc in next 3 chs, ch 1, dc in next 2 chs, dc in next dc, ch 5, skip next 2 chs, dc in next 3 chs, dc in next 4 dc, dc in next 3 chs, ch 5, skip next 2 dc, dc in next 6 dc, (ch 2, skip next ch-2 sp, dc in next dc) twice, ch 2, skip next 2 chs, dc in next ch: 47 dc, 2 ch-5 sps, 3 ch-2 sps and 1 ch-1 sp; ch 5, turn.

Row 15: Skip first dc, dc in next dc, (ch 2, skip next ch-2 sp, dc in next dc) twice, dc in next 3 dc, ch 5, skip next 2 chs, dc in next 3 chs, dc in next 10 dc, dc in next 3 chs, ch 5, skip next 2 dc, dc in next dc, dc in next ch, dc in next 2 dc, ch 8, skip next 6 dc, sl st in next dc: 27 dc, 1 ch-8 sp, 2 ch-5 sps and 3 ch-2 sps; ch 1, turn.

Rep Rows 2 through 15 for desired length. Finish off; weave in ends.

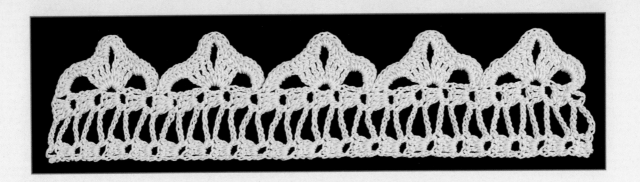

Ladders

Instructions

Ch 15.

Row 1 (wrong side): Dc in 4th ch from hook (skipped chs count as dc), dc in next 2 chs, ch 5, skip next 5 chs, sc in next ch, ch 2, skip next 2 chs, sc in last ch: 4 dc, 2 sc and 2 ch-sps; ch 3 (counts as dc on following row now and throughout), turn.

Row 2 (right side): Work 3 dc in ch-2 sp, ch 5, sc in next dc, ch 2, sc in top of turning ch; ch 3, turn.

Rows 3 through 6: Rep Row 2, 4 more times.

Row 7: Work 3 dc in ch-2 sp, ch 5, sc in next dc, ch 2, sc in top of turning ch; pivot piece to work along side edge, ch 4, skip 2 rows (4 tr, ch 4, 4 tr) in ch-sp at edge of next row, ch 4, skip 2 rows, sl st in edge of sc on next row: 8 tr, 4 dc, 2 sc and 5 ch-sps; ch 1, turn.

Row 8: Work 7 hdc in first ch-4 sp, (hdc in next 4 tr, 7 hdc in next ch-4 sp) twice, 4 dc in next ch-2 sp, ch 5, sc in next dc, ch 2, sc in top of turning ch: 4 dc, 29 hdc, 2 sc and 2 ch-sps; ch 3, turn.

Row 9: Work 3 dc in ch-2 sp, ch 5, sc in next dc, ch 2, skip next 2 dc, sc in next dc: 4 dc, 2 sc and 2 ch-sps; ch 3, turn, leaving rem sts along side edge unworked.

Rep Rows 2 through 9 for desired length, ending with a Row 8 rep. Finish off; weave in ends.

Lacy Triples

CHAIN MULTIPLE: 6 + 2

STITCH GUIDE

Tr shell (triple shell): Work (tr, ch 2, tr, ch 3, tr, ch 2, tr) in specified ch-sp: tr shell made.

Beg tr shell (beginning triple shell): Work (tr, ch 3, tr, ch 2, tr) in specified ch-sp: beg tr shell made.

Instructions

Ch a multiple of 6 chs plus 2 additional chs.

Row 1 (right side): Dc in 6th ch from hook; *ch 2, skip next 2 chs, dc in next ch; rep from * across to last 2 chs, ch 1, skip next ch, dc in last ch; ch 6 (counts as tr and ch-2 sp on following row), turn.

Row 2: Skip ch-1 sp; *tr in next ch-2 sp, ch 2; rep from * across to turning ch; skip next ch, tr in next ch; ch 6, turn.

Row 3: Work beg tr shell in next ch-2 sp; *skip next ch-2 sp, tr shell in next ch-2 sp; rep from * across to last 2 ch-2 sps; skip next ch-2 sp, tr shell in last ch-2 sp, working last tr of tr shell in 4th ch of turning ch-6. Finish off; weave in ends.

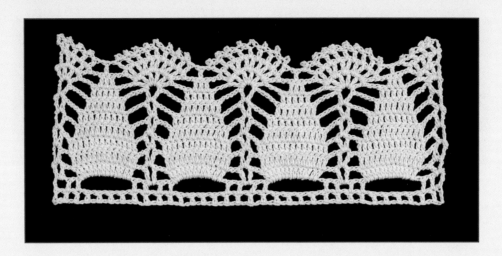

Pinecones

CHAIN MULTIPLE: 16 + 6

STITCH GUIDE

Beg V-st (beginning V-stitch): Work (sl st, ch 5, dc) in first ch-2 sp: beg V-st made.

V-st (V-stitch): Work (dc, ch 2, dc) in specified st or sp: V-st made.

Picot: Ch 3, sl st in 3rd ch from hook: picot made.

Instructions

Ch a multiple of 16 chs plus 6 additional chs.

Row 1 (right side): Dc in 6th ch from hook; *ch 1, skip next ch, dc in next ch; rep from * across; ch 4, turn.

Row 2: Skip first dc, dc in next dc, ch 1, dc in next dc; *ch 9, skip next 4 dc, dc in next dc**, (ch 1, dc in next dc) 3 times; rep from * across, ending last rep at **; ch 1, dc in next dc, ch 1, skip next ch, dc in next ch; turn.

Row 3: Sl st in first dc, work beg V-st; *ch 2, skip next ch-1 sp, 13 dc in next ch-9 sp, ch 2, skip next ch-1 sp**, (dc, ch 2, dc) in next ch-1 sp; rep from * across, ending last rep at **; (dc, ch 2, dc) in turning ch-4 sp; turn.

Rows 4 and 5: Sl st in first dc, work beg V-st; *ch 2, skip next ch-2 sp, dc in next 13 dc, ch 2, skip next ch-2 sp, V-st in ch-2 sp of next V-st; rep from * across; turn.

Row 6: Sl st in first dc, work beg V-st; *ch 3, skip next ch-2 sp, skip next dc, dc in next 11 dc, ch 3, skip next ch-2 sp, V-st in ch-2 sp of next V-st; rep from * across; turn.

Row 7: Sl st in first dc, work beg V-st; *ch 4, skip next ch-3 sp, skip next dc, dc in next 9 dc, ch 4, skip next ch-3 sp, V-st in ch-2 sp of next V-st; rep from * across; turn.

Row 8: Sl st in first dc, work beg V-st; *ch 5, skip next ch-4 sp, skip next dc, dc in next 7 dc, ch 5, skip next ch-4 sp**, (dc, ch 3, dc) in ch-2 sp of next V-st; rep from * across, ending last rep at **; V-st in ch-2 sp of last V-st; turn.

Row 9: Sl st in first dc, (sl st, ch 4, dc, ch 1, dc, ch 1, dc) in ch-2 sp of first V-st; *ch 3, skip next ch-5 sp, skip next dc, dc in next 5 dc, ch 3, skip next ch-5 sp**, (dc, ch 1) 5 times in next ch-3 sp, dc in same ch-3 sp; rep from * across, ending last rep at **; (dc, ch 1) 3 times in turning ch-sp, dc in same ch-sp; turn.

Row 10: Sl st in first dc, sl st in next ch-1 sp, ch 4, (dc, ch 1, dc) in next ch-1 sp, ch 1, (dc, ch 1, dc) in next ch-1 sp; *ch 2, skip next ch-3 sp, skip next dc, dc in next 3 dc, ch 2, skip next ch-3 sp**, (dc, ch 1) twice in each of next 4 ch-1 sps, (dc, ch 1, dc) in next ch-1 sp; rep from * across, ending last rep at **; (dc, ch 1) twice in each of next 2 ch-1 sps, dc in turning ch-sp; ch 3, turn.

Row 11: Work picot, (dc in next ch-1 sp, picot) 3 times, dc in next ch-1 sp; *ch 1, skip next ch-2 sp, dc in next dc, ch 1, skip next ch-2 sp**, (dc in next ch-1 sp, picot) 8 times, dc in next ch-1 sp; rep from * across, ending last rep at **; (dc in next ch-1 sp, picot) 4 times, dc in 3rd ch of turning ch-4. Finish off; weave in ends.

Lacy Shells

STITCH GUIDE

4-tr shell (4 triple crochet shell): Work [(tr, ch 2) 3 times, tr] in specified st or sp: 4-tr shell made.

6-tr shell (6 triple crochet shell): Work [(tr, ch 2) 5 times, tr] in specified st or sp: 6-tr shell made.

Instructions

Ch 7.

Row 1 (wrong side): Work 4-tr shell in 7th ch from hook: one 4-tr shell; ch 1, turn.

Row 2 (right side): Work (2 sc, ch 2, 2 sc) in each ch-2 sp on 4-tr shell: 12 sc and 3 ch-2 sps; ch 6, turn.

Row 3: Skip first ch-2 sp, 4-tr shell in next ch-2 sp: one 4-tr shell; ch 1, turn.

Row 4: Rep Row 2.

Row 5: Skip first ch-2 sp, 4-tr shell in next ch-2 sp, skip next ch-2 sp; working along side edge, 6-tr shell in turning ch-1 sp, skip next row, sl st in next ch-2 sp on next row: one 6-tr shell and one 4-tr shell; ch 1, turn.

Row 6: Work (2 sc, ch 2, 2 sc) in each ch-2 sp on 6-tr shell, (2 sc, ch 2, 2 sc) in each ch-2 sp on 4-tr shell: 32 sc and 8 ch-2 sps; ch 6, turn.

Rep Rows 3 through 6 for desired length. Do NOT ch at end of last row. Finish off; weave in ends.

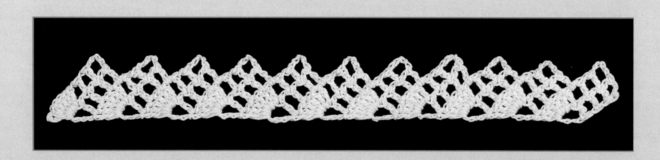

Diagonal Edge

Instructions

Ch 10.

Row 1 (wrong side): Dc in 6th ch from hook, ch 1, skip next ch, dc in next ch, ch 1, skip next ch, (dc, ch 1, dc) in last ch: 4 dc and 4 ch-sps; ch 4, turn.

Row 2 (right side): Skip first dc, dc in next dc, (ch 1, dc in next dc) twice, 5 dc in turning ch-sp: 8 dc and 3 ch-sps; ch 5, turn.

Row 3: Dc in first dc, (ch 1, skip next dc, dc in next dc) twice, ch 1, skip next dc, dc in next ch-1 sp: 4 dc and 4 ch-sps; ch 4, turn, leaving rem sts unworked.

Rep Rows 2 and 3 for desired length, ending with a Row 2 rep. Finish off; weave in ends.

Ovals

CHAIN MULTIPLE: 10 + 3

STITCH GUIDE

7-tr cl (7 triple crochet cluster): *YO twice, insert hook in next tr and draw up a lp, (YO and draw through 2 lps on hook) twice; rep from * 6 more times; YO and draw through all 8 lps on hook: 7-tr cl made.

Picot: Ch 7, sc in 7th ch from hook: picot made.

Instructions

Ch a multiple of 10 chs plus 3 additional chs.

Row 1 (wrong side): Sc in 2nd ch from hook; *ch 5, sc in next 5 chs; rep from * across to last ch; ch 5, sc in last ch: odd number of ch-5 sps; turn.

Row 2 (right side): Sl st in first sc, sl st in first 2 chs of next ch-5 sp, ch 1, 2 sc in same ch-5 sp; *ch 3, 7 tr in next ch-5 sp, ch 3**, 3 sc in next ch-5 sp; rep from * across, ending last rep at **; 2 sc in last ch-5 sp; ch 1, turn.

Row 3: Sc in first sc; *ch 7, work 7-tr cl over next 7 tr, ch 7, skip next sc, sc in next sc; rep from * across; ch 1, turn.

Row 4: *Work 7 sc in next ch-7 sp, 3 picots, 7 sc in next ch-7 sp; rep from * across; sl st in last sc. Finish off; weave in ends.

Waves

STITCH GUIDE

Shell: Work (3 dc, ch 2, 3 dc) in specified st or sp: shell made.

Instructions

Row 1 (right side): Ch 9, shell in 6th ch from hook, skip next 2 chs, dc in last ch: 1 shell and 1 dc; ch 4, turn.

Row 2: Shell in ch-sp of shell, ch 4, dc in turning ch-sp of Row 1: 1 shell, 1 dc and 1 ch-4 sp; ch 3, turn.

Row 3: Work 5 dc in ch-4 sp, ch 1, shell in ch-sp of shell, tr in turning ch-sp: 1 shell, 1 tr and 5 dc; ch 4, turn.

Row 4: Shell in ch-sp of shell, ch 2, skip next ch-1 sp, (dc in next dc, ch 2) 5 times, dc in top of turning ch: 1 shell, 6 dc and 6 ch-2 sps; ch 5, turn.

Row 5: Sc in next ch-2 sp, (ch 5, sc in next ch-2 sp) 4 times, ch 3, shell in ch-sp of shell, tr in turning ch-sp: 1 shell, 1 tr, 5 sc and 5 ch-5 sps; ch 4, turn.

Row 6: Shell in ch-sp of shell, ch 4, skip next 2 dc, dc in next dc: 1 shell, 1 dc and 1 ch-4 sp; ch 3, turn.

Rep Rows 3 through 6 for desired length. At end of last row, do not ch 3. Finish off; weave in ends.

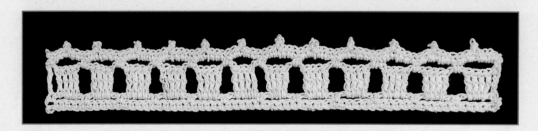

Blocks and Picots

CHAIN MULTIPLE: 5 + 2

STITCH GUIDE

Picot: Ch 3, sl st in 3rd ch from hook: picot made.

Instructions

Ch a multiple of 5 chs plus 2 additional chs.

Row 1 (right side): Sc in 2nd ch from hook and in each rem ch across: multiple of 5 sc + 1 sc; ch 1, turn.

Row 2: Sc in first sc; *ch 5, skip next 4 sc, sc in next sc; rep from * across; ch 5, turn.

Row 3: Work 4 tr in first ch-5 sp; *ch 3, 4 tr in next ch-5 sp; rep from * across; ch 1, tr in last sc; ch 1, turn.

Row 4: Sc in first tr; *ch 5, skip next 4 tr, sc in next ch-3 sp; rep from * across, working last sc in 4th ch of turning ch-5; ch 1, turn.

Row 5: Sc in first sc, (3 sc, picot, 3 sc) in each ch-5 sp across; sc in last sc. Finish off; weave in ends.

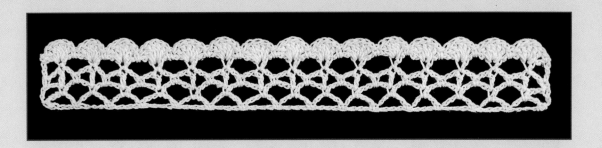

Tulips

CHAIN MULTIPLE: 4 + 2

Instructions

Ch a multiple of 4 chs plus 2 additional chs.

Row 1 (right side): Sc in 2nd ch from hook; *ch 5, skip next 3 chs, sc in next ch; rep from * across; ch 5, turn.

Row 2: Sc in first ch-5 sp; *ch 5, sc in next ch-5 sp; rep from * across; ch 2, dc in last sc; ch 1, turn.

Row 3: Sc in first dc; *ch 2, dc in next sc, ch 2, sc in next ch-5 sp; rep from * across, working last sc in 3rd ch of turning ch-5; ch 5, turn.

Row 4: Sc in first dc; *ch 5, sc in next dc; rep from * across; ch 2, dc in last sc; ch 1, turn.

Row 5: Sc in first dc; *5 dc in next sc, sc in next ch-5 sp; rep from * across, working last sc in 3rd ch of turning ch-5. Finish off; weave in ends.

Semi-Circles

CHAIN MULTIPLE: 14 + 6

Instructions

Ch a multiple of 14 chs plus 6 additional chs.

Row 1 (wrong side): Sc in 8th ch from hook; *ch 2, skip next 4 chs, [(tr, ch 2) 4 times] in next ch, skip next 4 chs, sc in next ch**, ch 5, skip next 3 chs, sc in next ch; rep from * across, ending last rep at **; ch 2, skip next ch, dc in last ch; ch 1, turn.

Row 2 (right side): Sc in first dc; *skip next sc, 4 dc in each of next 4 dc, skip next sc**, sc in next ch-5 sp; rep from * across, ending last rep at **; skip next 2 chs, sc in next ch. Finish off; weave in ends.

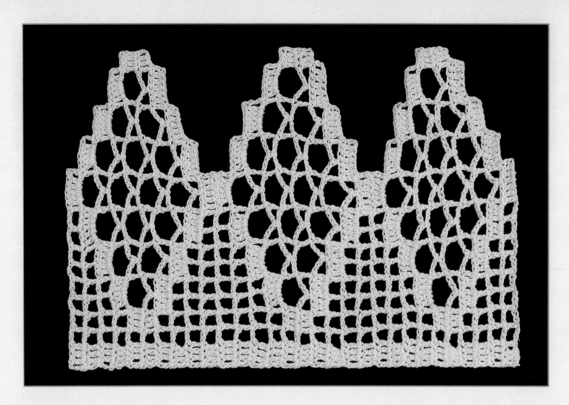

Filet Diamonds

STITCH GUIDE

Fdc (foundation double crochet): YO, insert hook in specified st and draw up a lp, YO and draw through one lp on hook (counts as ch at base of fdc), (YO and draw through 2 lps on hook) twice: fdc made.

Instructions

Ch 36.

Row 1 (right side): Dc in 4th ch from hook (skipped chs count as dc), dc in next 5 chs, (ch 2, skip next 2 chs, dc in next ch) 8 times, dc in last 3 chs: 18 dc and 8 ch-2 sps; ch 3 (counts as dc on following row now and throughout), turn.

Row 2: Skip first dc, dc in next 3 dc, (ch 2, skip next ch-2 sp, dc in next dc) 6 times, (2 dc in next ch-2 sp, dc in next dc) twice, ch 3, skip next 2 dc, sc in next dc, ch 3, skip next 2 dc, dc in top of turning ch, fdc in same ch as last dc, (fdc in ch at base of last fdc made) 5 times: 6 fdc, 17 dc, 2 ch-3 sps and 6 ch-2 sps; ch 8 (counts as dc and 5 chs), turn.

Row 3: Dc in 4th ch from hook, dc in next 4 chs, dc in next fdc, ch 3, skip next 2 fdc, sc in next fdc, ch 3, skip next 2 fdc, dc in next dc, ch 5, skip next 2 ch-3 sps, dc in next dc, ch 3, skip next 2 dc, sc in next dc, ch 3, skip next 2 dc, dc in next dc, (2 dc in next ch-2 sp, dc in next dc) twice, (ch 2, skip next ch-2 sp, dc in next dc) 4 times, dc in next 2 dc, dc in top of turning ch: 23 dc, 1 ch-5 sp, 4 ch-3 sps and 4 ch-2 sps; ch 3, turn.

Row 4: Skip first dc, dc in next 3 dc, (ch 2, skip next ch-2 sp, dc in next dc) twice, (2 dc in next ch-2 sp, dc in next dc) twice; *ch 3, skip next 2 dc, sc in next dc, ch 3, skip next 2 dc**, dc in next dc; †ch 5, skip next 2 ch-3 sps, dc in next dc††, ch 3, skip next 2 chs, sc in next ch, ch 3, skip next 2 chs, dc in next dc; rep from † to †† once; rep from * to ** once; dc in top of turning ch, fdc in same ch as last dc, (fdc in ch at base of last fdc made) 5 times: 6 fdc, 17 dc, 2 ch-5 sps, 6 ch-3 sps and 2 ch-2 sps; ch 5 (counts as dc and 2 chs), turn.

Row 5: Dc in 4th ch from hook, dc in next ch, dc in next fdc, ch 3, skip next 2 fdc, sc in next fdc, ch 3, skip next 2 fdc, dc in next dc; (*ch 5, skip next 2 ch-3 sps, dc in next dc**, ch 3, skip next 2 chs, sc in next ch, ch 3, skip next 2 chs, dc in next dc) twice; rep from * to ** once; ch 3, skip next 2 dc, sc in next dc, ch 3, skip next 2 dc, dc in next dc, 2 dc in next ch-2 sp, dc in next dc, ch 2, skip next ch-2 sp, dc in next 3 dc, dc in top of turning ch: 18 dc, 3 ch-5 sps, 8 ch-3 sps and 1 ch-2 sp; ch 3, turn.

Row 6: Skip first dc, dc in next 3 dc, ch 2, skip next ch-2 sp, dc in next 4 dc; (*ch 5, skip next 2 ch-3 sps, dc in next dc**, ch 3, skip next 2 chs, sc in next ch, ch 3, skip next 2 chs, dc in next dc) 3 times; rep from * to ** once; dc in next 2 dc, dc in top of turning ch: 18 dc, 4 ch-5 sps, 6 ch-3 sps and 1 ch-2 sp; turn.

Row 7: Sl st in first 4 dc, ch 3 (counts as dc), 5 dc in next ch-5 sp, dc in next dc; (*ch 5, skip next 2 ch-3 sps, dc in next dc**, ch 3, skip next 2 chs, sc in next ch, ch 3, skip next 2 chs, dc in next dc) twice; rep from * to ** once; 5 dc in next ch-5 sp, dc in next dc, ch 2, skip next 2 dc, dc in next dc, ch 2, skip next ch-2 sp, dc in next 3 dc, dc in top of turning ch: 23 dc, 3 ch-5 sps, 4 ch-3 sps and 2 ch-2 sps; ch 3, turn.

Row 8: Skip first dc, dc in next 3 dc, (ch 2, skip next ch-2 sp, dc in next dc) twice, (ch 2, skip next 2 dc, dc in next dc) twice, 5 dc in next ch-5 sp, dc in next dc, ch 5, skip next 2 ch-3 sps, dc in next dc, ch 3, skip next 2 chs, sc in next ch, ch 3, skip next 2 chs, dc in next dc, ch 5, skip next 2 ch-3 sps, dc in next dc, 5 dc in next ch-5 sp, dc in next dc: 23 dc, 2 ch-5 sps, 2 ch-3 sps and 4 ch-2 sps; turn.

Row 9: Sl st in first 7 dc, ch 3 (counts as dc), 5 dc in next ch-5 sp, dc in next dc, ch 5, skip next 2 ch-3 sps, dc in next dc, 5 dc in next ch-5 sp, dc in next dc, (ch 2, skip next 2 dc, dc in next dc) twice, (ch 2, skip next ch-2 sp, dc in next dc) 4 times, dc in next 2 dc, dc in top of turning ch: 23 dc, 1 ch-5 sp and 6 ch-2 sps; ch 3, turn.

Row 10: Skip first dc, dc in next 3 dc, (ch 2, skip next ch-2 sp, dc in next dc) 6 times, (ch 2, skip next 2 dc, dc in next dc) twice, 5 dc in next ch-5 sp, dc in next dc: 18 dc and 8 ch-2 sps; ch 3, turn.

Row 11: Skip first dc, dc in next 6 dc, (ch 2, skip next ch-2 sp, dc in next dc) 8 times, dc in next 2 dc, dc in top of turning ch: 18 dc and 8 ch-2 sps; ch 3, turn.

Rep Rows 2 through 11 until desired length, ending by working a Row 10 rep. Finish off; weave in ends.

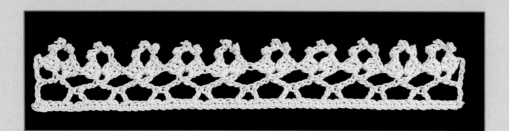

Picot Shells

CHAIN MULTIPLE: 6 + 1

STITCH GUIDE

Picot: Ch 3, sc in 3rd ch from hook: picot made.

Picot shell: Work (3 dc, 3 picots, 3 dc) in specified st or sp: picot shell made.

Instructions

Ch a multiple of 6 chs plus 1 additional ch.

Row 1 (right side): Sc in 2nd ch from hook and in each rem ch across; ch 11 (first 3 chs count as dc on following row), turn.

Row 2: Sc in 6th ch from hook (forms a ch-5 sp), ch 2, skip first 4 sc in Row 1, dc in next sc; *skip next 2 sc, dc in next sc, ch 8, sc in 6th ch from hook (forms a ch-5 sp), ch 2**, skip next 2 sc, dc in next sc; rep from * across, ending last rep at **; skip next 3 sc, dc in last sc; ch 4 (counts as tr on following row), turn.

Row 3: *Work picot shell in next ch-5 sp; rep from * across, tr in 3rd ch of turning ch-11. Finish off; weave in ends.

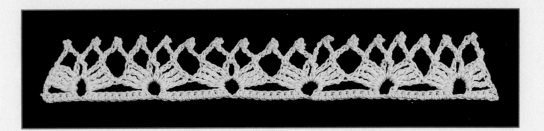

Wings

CHAIN MULTIPLE: 10 + 1

STITCH GUIDE

Picot: Ch 4, sc in 4th ch from hook: picot made.

Instructions

Ch a multiple of 10 chs plus 1 additional ch.

Row 1 (wrong side): Sc in 2nd ch from hook and in next 4 chs, ch 6; *sc in next 10 chs, ch 6; rep from * across to last 5 chs, sc in last 5 chs; ch 1, turn.

Row 2 (right side): *In next ch-6 sp work (3 tr, ch 4, sc, ch 5, sc, ch 4, 3 tr); rep from * across, ch 1, sl st in first sc on Row 1; turn.

Row 3: Sl st in ch-1 sp, sl st in next 3 tr; *sc in top ch of next ch-4, ch 2, picot, ch 2, sc in next ch-5 sp, ch 2, picot, ch 2, sc in top ch of next ch-4**, ch 2, picot, ch 2; rep from * across, ending last rep at **. Finish off; weave in ends.

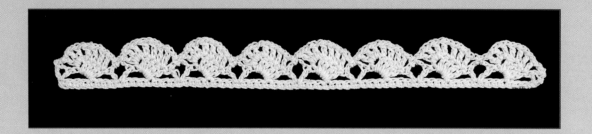

Shell Blocks

CHAIN MULTIPLE: 8 + 2

STITCH GUIDE

V-st (V-stitch): Work (dc, ch 3, dc) in specified st or sp: V-st made.

Instructions

Ch a multiple of 8 chs plus 2 additional chs.

Row 1 (right side): Sc in 2nd ch from hook and in each rem ch across; ch 4, turn.

Row 2: Dc in first sc; *skip next 3 sc, dc in next sc, ch 3, work 4 dc around post of last dc made, skip next 3 sc**, V-st in next sc; rep from * across, ending last rep at **; (dc, ch 1, dc) in last sc; ch 1, turn.

Row 3: Sc in first dc; *ch 1, skip next dc, (dc in next dc, ch 1) 4 times, [(dc, ch 1) 3 times] over ch-3 below last dc just worked, skip next dc**, sc in ch-3 sp of next V-st; rep from * across, ending last rep at **; sc in 3rd ch of turning ch-4. Finish off; weave in ends.

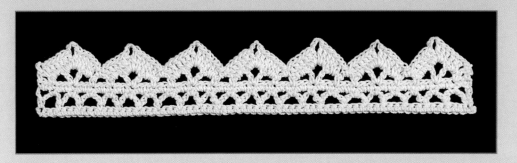

Pyramids

CHAIN MULTIPLE: 9 + 2

Instructions

Ch a multiple of 9 chs plus 2 additional chs.

Row 1 (wrong side): Sc in 2nd ch from hook and in each rem ch across; ch 1, turn.

Row 2 (right side): Sc in first sc; *ch 5, skip next 2 sc, sc in next sc; rep from * across; ch 4, turn.

Row 3: Sc in next ch-5 sp; *ch 2, sc in next ch-5 sp; rep from * across; ch 1, dc in last sc; ch 1, turn.

Row 4: Sc in first dc, sc in next ch-1 sp, sc in next sc; *2 sc in next ch-2 sp, sc in next sc; rep from * across to turning chs; sc in turning ch-4 sp, sc in 3rd ch of turning ch-4; ch 3, turn.

Row 5: Skip first 2 sc, sc in next sc; *ch 2, skip next 2 sc, (dc, ch 3, dc) in next sc, ch 2, skip next 2 sc, sc in next sc**, ch 3, skip next 2 sc, sc in next sc; rep from * across, ending last rep at **; ch 1, skip next sc, hdc in last sc; ch 1, turn.

Row 6: Sc in hdc; *2 dc in next ch-2 sp, dc in next dc, (3 dc, ch 3, 3 dc) in next ch-3 sp, dc in next dc, 2 dc in next ch-2 sp**, sc in next ch-3 sp; rep from * across, ending last rep at **; sc in 2nd ch of turning ch-3. Finish off; weave in ends.

Shells

CHAIN MULTIPLE: 18 + 5

STITCH GUIDE

Shell: Work [(tr, ch 1) 7 times, tr] in specified st or sp: shell made.

Picot: Ch 4, sc in 4th ch from hook: picot made.

Instructions

Ch a multiple of 18 chs plus 5 additional chs.

Row 1 (wrong side): Dc in 6th ch from hook; *ch 2, skip next 2 chs, dc in next ch; rep from * across to last 2 chs; ch 1, skip next ch, dc in last ch; ch 1, turn.

Row 2 (right side): Sc in first dc, ch 3, skip next ch-1 sp, sc in next ch-2 sp; *ch 2, skip next ch-2 sp, shell in next ch-2 sp, ch 2, skip next ch-2 sp, sc in next ch-2 sp**, (ch 3, sc in next ch-2 sp) twice; rep from * across, ending last rep at **; ch 3, skip next dc and next ch, sc in next ch; ch 3, turn.

Row 3: Sc in next ch-3 sp; *skip next ch-2 sp, (ch 3, sc in next ch-1 sp) 7 times, skip next ch-2 sp**, (ch 3, sc in next ch-3 sp) twice; rep from * across, ending last rep at **; ch 3, sc in next ch-3 sp, ch 1, hdc in last sc; ch 1, turn.

Row 4: Sc in first hdc; *ch 4, skip next ch-3 sp, (sc in next ch-3 sp, ch 1, picot, ch 1) 5 times, sc in next ch-3 sp, ch 4, skip next ch-3 sp**, sc in next ch-3 sp; rep from * across, ending last rep at **; sc in 2nd ch of turning ch-3. Finish off; weave in ends.

V-Stitch Shells

CHAIN MULTIPLE: 6 + 2

STITCH GUIDE

V-st (V-stitch): Work (dc, ch 2, dc) in specified st or sp: V-st made.

Shell: Work [(tr, ch 2) 4 times, tr] in specified st or sp: shell made.

Instructions

Ch a multiple of 6 chs plus 2 additional chs.

Row 1 (wrong side): Sc in 2nd ch from hook and in each rem ch across; ch 4, turn.

Row 2 (right side): Dc in first sc; *ch 3, skip next 5 sc, V-st in next sc; rep from * across to last 6 sc; ch 3, skip next 5 sc, (dc, ch 1, dc) in last sc; ch 4, turn.

Row 3: Dc in first dc; *skip next ch-3 sp, shell in ch-2 sp of next V-st, skip next ch-3 sp**, V-st in ch-2 sp of next V-st; rep from * across, ending last rep at **; (dc, ch 1, dc) in 3rd ch of turning ch-4; ch 1, turn.

Row 4: Sc in first dc, skip next ch-1 sp; *ch 3, sc in next ch-2 sp; rep from * across to turning ch-4 sp; ch 3, sc in 3rd ch of turning ch-4. Finish off; weave in ends.

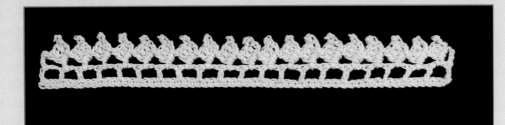

Small Diagonal Blocks

CHAIN MULTIPLE: 3 + 2

STITCH GUIDE

Picot: Ch 3, sl st in 3rd ch from hook: picot made.

Instructions

Ch a multiple of 3 chs plus 2 additional chs.

Row 1 (right side): Sc in 2nd ch from hook and in each rem ch across; ch 5, turn.

Row 2: Skip first 3 sc, dc in next sc; *ch 2, skip next 2 sc, dc in next sc; rep from * across; ch 3, turn.

Row 3: Dc in first ch-2 sp; *ch 2, picot, 3 dc around post of last dc made**, dc in next ch-2 sp; rep from * across, ending last rep at **; dc in 3rd ch of turning ch-5. Finish off; weave in ends.

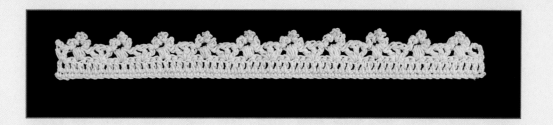

Puff Stitches

CHAIN MULTIPLE: 6 + 2

STITCH GUIDE

Puff st (puff stitch): (YO, insert hook in specified st and draw up a lp to height of a dc) 4 times, YO and draw through all 9 lps on hook, ch 1 tightly to secure st: puff st made.

Triple picot: (Ch 3, sl st, ch 4, sl st, ch 3, sl st) in lp that closed puff st: triple picot made.

Instructions

Ch a multiple of 6 chs plus 2 additional chs.

Row 1 (right side): Sc in 2nd ch from hook and in each rem ch across; ch 3, turn.

Row 2: Skip first sc, dc in next sc and in each rem sc across; ch 4, turn.

Row 3: Dc in first dc; *skip next 2 dc, puff st in next dc, work triple picot, skip next 2 dc**, (dc, ch 1, dc, ch 1, dc) in next dc; rep from * across, ending last rep at **; (dc, ch 1, dc) in last dc. Finish off; weave in ends.

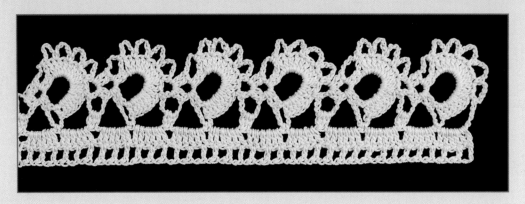

Curves

STITCH GUIDE

Dc-cl (double crochet cluster): (YO, insert hook in specified st or sp and draw up a lp, YO and draw through 2 lps on hook) 3 times, YO and draw through all 4 lps on hook: dc-cl made.

Instructions

Ch 8.

Row 1 (right side): Work (2 dc, ch 3, 2 dc) in 8th ch from hook: 4 dc, 1 ch-7 sp and 1 ch-3 sp; ch 7, turn.

Row 2: Work (2 dc, ch 10, 2 dc) in ch-3 sp: 4 dc, 1 ch-7 sp and 1 ch-10 sp; ch 5, turn.

Row 3: Work 17 dc in ch-10 sp, sc in ch-6 sp: 17 dc and 1 sc; ch 5, turn.

Row 4: Skip first dc, sc in next dc, (ch 5, skip next dc, sc in next dc) 4 times: 5 sc and 5 ch-5 sps; ch 7, turn.

Row 5: Skip first sc, (2 dc, ch 3, 2 dc) in next ch-5 sp: 4 dc, 1 ch-7 sp and 1 ch-3 sp; ch 7, turn.

Rep Rows 2 through 5 for desired length, ending by working a Row 4 rep. Ch 9 at end of last row instead of ch 7. Do NOT finish off and do NOT turn.

Edge

Row 1 (wrong side): Sc in ch-5 sp at edge of next row; *ch 5, dc-cl in ch-7 sp at edge of next row**, ch 5, sc in ch-5 sp at edge of next row; rep from * across, ending last rep at **; ch 3, turn.

Row 2 (right side): Work 6 dc in each ch-5 sp across, ending with 6 dc in turning ch-9 sp; ch 4, turn.

Row 3: Skip first 2 dc; *dc in next dc, ch 1, skip next dc; rep from * across to turning ch; dc in top of turning ch-3. Finish off; weave in ends.

Fountains

CHAIN MULTIPLE: 22 + 3

Instructions

Ch a multiple of 22 chs plus 3 additional chs.

Row 1 (right side): Sc in 2nd ch from hook and in each rem ch across; ch 3, turn.

Row 2: Skip first sc, dc in next sc; *ch 3, skip next 2 sc, sc in next sc, (ch 5, skip next 2 sc, sc in next sc) 5 times, ch 3, skip next 2 sc, dc in next 2 sc; rep from * across; ch 3 (counts as dc on following row now and throughout), turn.

Row 3: Dc in first dc, 2 dc in next dc; *ch 4, skip next ch-3 sp, sc in next ch-5 sp, (ch 5, sc in next ch-5 sp) 4 times, ch 4, skip next ch-3 sp, 2 dc in each of next 2 dc; rep from * across; ch 3, turn.

Row 4: Dc in first dc, dc in next 2 dc, 2 dc in next dc; *skip next ch-4 sp, (ch 5, sc in next ch-5 sp) 4 times, ch 5, skip next ch-4 sp, 2 dc in next dc, dc in next 2 dc, 2 dc in next dc; rep from * across; ch 3, turn.

Row 5: Dc in first dc, dc in next 4 dc, 2 dc in next dc; *skip next ch-5 sp, (ch 5, sc in next ch-5 sp) 3 times, ch 5, skip next ch-5 sp, 2 dc in next dc, dc in next 4 dc, 2 dc in next dc; rep from * across; ch 4 (counts as dc and ch-1 sp on following row), turn.

Row 6: Dc in first dc, (ch 1, dc in next dc) 6 times, ch 1, (dc, ch 1, dc) in next dc; *skip next ch-5 sp, (ch 5, sc in next ch-5 sp) twice, ch 5, skip next ch-5 sp, (dc, ch 1, dc) in next dc, (ch 1, dc in next dc) 6 times, ch 1, (dc, ch 1, dc) in next dc; rep from * across; ch 1, turn.

Row 7: Sc in first dc, (ch 2, sc in next ch-1 sp) 9 times, ch 2, sc in next dc; *ch 7, skip next ch-5 sp, sc in next ch-5 sp, ch 7, sc in next dc, (ch 2, sc in next ch-1 sp) 9 times, ch 2**, sc in next dc; rep from * across, ending last rep at **; sc in 3rd ch of turning ch-4. Finish off; weave in ends.

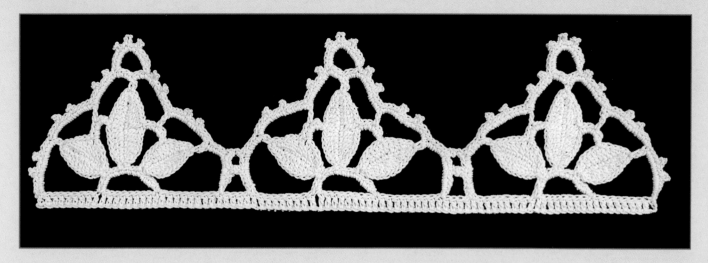

Leaves

CHAIN MULTIPLE: 31 + 29

STITCH GUIDE

Picot: Ch 3, sl st in top of last sc made before ch-3: picot made.

Picot join: Ch 1, sl st in adjacent picot made on previous edging, ch 1, sl st in top of last sc made before first ch-1: picot join made.

Instructions

Ch a multiple of 31 chs plus 29 additional chs.

First Group of 3 Leaves

Dc in 4th ch from hook (skipped chs count as first dc), dc in next 16 chs; ch 10, turn; sl st in 8th dc before last dc made, turn; 4 sc in ch-10 sp.

First Leaf

Ch 9, sc in 2nd ch from hook and in next 7 chs (stem made); rotate piece; working in free lps on opposite side of chs along stem, sc in first ch, hdc in next ch, dc in next ch, 2 dc in each of next 2 chs, dc in next ch, hdc in next ch, sc in next ch, 3 sc in skipped ch at tip of stem; working in sc on opposite side of stem, sc in first sc, hdc in next sc, dc in next sc, 2 dc in next sc (place stitch marker in 2nd of these 2 dc), 2 dc in next sc, dc in next sc, hdc in next sc, sc in last sc; sl st in last sc made before leaf, 3 sc in ch-10 sp.

Second Leaf

Ch 12, sc in 2nd ch from hook and in next 10 chs (stem made); rotate piece; working in free lps on opposite side of chs along stem, sc in first ch, hdc in next ch, dc in next 2 chs, 2 dc in each of next 2 chs, ch 4, turn; sl st in marked st on first leaf, turn; 5 sc in ch-4 sp; working along stem again, 2 dc in next ch, dc in next 2 chs, hdc in next ch, sc in next ch, 3 sc in skipped ch at tip of stem; working in sc on opposite side of stem, sc in first sc, hdc in next sc, dc in next 2 sc, 2 dc in each of next 3 sc (insert stitch marker in 3rd dc), dc in next 2 sc, hdc in next sc, sc in last sc; sl st in sc made before leaf, 3 sc in ch-10 sp.

Third Leaf

Ch 9, sc in 2nd ch from hook and in next 7 chs (stem made); rotate piece; working in free lps on opposite side of chs along stem, sc in first ch, hdc in next ch, dc in next ch, 2 dc in next ch, ch 4, turn; sl st in marked st on second leaf, turn; 5 sc in ch-4 sp; working along stem again, 2 dc in next ch, dc in next ch, hdc in next ch, sc in next ch, 3 sc in skipped ch at tip of stem; working in sc on opposite side of stem, sc in first sc, hdc in next sc, dc in next sc, 2 dc in each of next 2 sc, dc in next sc, hdc in next sc, sc in last sc; sl st in last sc made before leaf, 3 sc in ch-10 sp.

Edging

Dc in next 9 chs, ch 9, turn; sc in sc at tip of third leaf, (ch 9, dc in center sc of 5 sc between leaves, ch 9, sc in sc at tip of next leaf) twice, ch 9, sc in 9th dc before group of 3 leaves; ch 1, turn; (4 sc, picot, 3 sc, picot, 4 sc) in each of first 3 ch-9 sps, 3 sc in next ch-9 sp; ch 8, turn; sl st in 5th sc before last sc worked, turn; (5 sc, picot, 2 sc, picot, 2 sc, picot, 5 sc) in ch-8 sp, (sc, picot, 3 sc, picot, 4 sc) in rem of ch-9 sp, (4 sc, picot, 3 sc, picot, 4 sc) in each of next 2 ch-9 sps, sl st in last dc made before first ch-9.

Second Group of 3 Leaves

Dc in next 22 chs; ch 10, turn; sl st in 8th dc before last dc made, turn; 4 sc in ch-10 sp.

Rep First, Second and Third Leaf.

Edging

Dc in next 9 chs, ch 9, turn; sc in center sc at tip of third leaf, (ch 9, dc in center sc of 5 sc between leaves, ch 9, sc in center sc at tip of next leaf) twice, ch 9, sc in 9th dc before group of 3 leaves; ch 1, turn; (4 sc, picot join, 3 sc, picot join, 4 sc) in first ch-9 sp, (4 sc, picot, 3 sc, picot, 4 sc) in each of next 2 ch-9 sps, 3 sc in next ch-9 sp; ch 8, turn; sl st in 5th sc before last sc worked, turn; (5 sc, picot, 2 sc, picot, 2 sc, picot, 5 sc) in ch-8 sp, (sc, picot, 3 sc, picot, 4 sc) in rem of ch-9 sp, (4 sc, picot, 3 sc, picot, 4 sc) in each of next 2 ch-9 sps, sl st in last dc made before first ch-9.

Work each additional group of 3 leaves same as Second Group of 3 Leaves. At end of last group of 3 leaves, finish off; weave in ends.

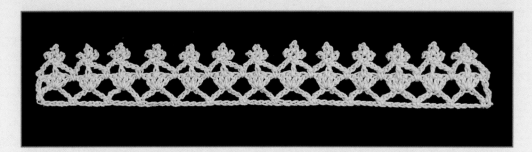

Little Flowers

CHAIN MULTIPLE: 5 + 2

STITCH GUIDE

Tr picot (triple picot): Ch 3, sl st in 3rd ch from hook, ch 4, sl st in 4th ch from hook, ch 3, sl st in 3rd ch from hook, sl st in top of last dc made before first ch-3: tr picot made.

Instructions

Ch a multiple of 5 chs plus 2 additional chs.

Row 1 (right side): Sc in 2nd ch from hook; *ch 7, skip next 4 chs, sc in next ch; rep from * across; ch 4, turn.

Row 2: Work 4 dc in 4th ch of first ch-7 sp; *ch 1, 4 dc in 4th ch of next ch-7 sp; rep from * across; tr in last sc; ch 1, turn.

Row 3: Sc in first tr; *ch 3, dc in sp between 2nd and 3rd dc of next 4-dc group, tr picot, ch 3**, sc in next ch-1 sp; rep from * across, ending last rep at **; sc in top of turning ch-4. Finish off; weave in ends.

Mountains and Sun Rays

CHAIN MULTIPLE: 13 + 5

STITCH GUIDE

Shell: Work (sc, hdc, 3 dc, hdc, sc) in specified ch-sp: shell made.

Cl (cluster): (YO, insert hook in specified ch-sp and draw up a lp, YO and draw through 2 lps on hook) 3 times, YO and draw through all 4 lps on hook: cl made.

Picot: Ch 4, sc in 4th ch from hook: picot made.

Instructions

Ch a multiple of 13 chs plus 5 additional chs.

Row 1 (wrong side): Sc in 2nd ch from hook and in each rem ch across; ch 1, turn.

Row 2 (right side): Sc in first sc; *ch 3, skip next 2 sc, sc in next sc**, (ch 5, skip next 4 sc, sc in next sc) twice; rep from * across, ending last rep at **; ch 4, turn.

Row 3: Dc in first ch-3 sp; *ch 2, shell in next ch-5 sp, ch 3, shell in next ch-5 sp, ch 2, dc in next ch-3 sp; rep from * across; ch 1, dc in last sc; ch 1, turn.

Row 4: Sc in first dc, skip next ch-1 sp; *ch 4, sc in next ch-2 sp, ch 7, shell in next ch-3 sp, ch 7, sc in next ch-2 sp; rep from * across; ch 4, sc in 3rd ch of turning ch-4; ch 4, turn.

Row 5: Cl in first ch-4 sp; *ch 5, sc in next ch-7 sp, ch 6, sc in next ch-7 sp, ch 5, cl in next ch-4 sp; rep from * across; ch 1, dc in last sc; ch 1, turn.

Row 6: Sc in first dc; *ch 4, sc in next ch-5 sp, ch 4, 11 sc in next ch-7 sp, ch 4, sc in next ch-5 sp; rep from * across; ch 4, sc in 3rd ch of turning ch-4; turn.

Row 7: Sl st in first 2 chs, ch 1, sc in same ch-4 sp, picot; *ch 3, skip next ch-4 sp, skip first 2 sc of 11 sc group, dc in next sc, (picot, dc in next sc) 6 times, ch 3, skip last 2 sc of 11 sc group, skip next ch-4 sp, sc in next ch-4 sp, picot; rep from * across; ch 1, sl st in same ch-4 sp. Finish off; weave in ends.

Fancy Fans

STITCH GUIDE

L-shell (large shell): Work (3 dc, ch 2, 3 dc) in specified st or sp: L-shell made.

M-shell (medium shell): Work (2 dc, ch 3, 2 dc) in specified st or sp: M-shell made.

S-shell (small shell): Work (2 dc, ch 2, 2 dc) in specified st or sp: S-shell made.

V-st (V-stitch): Work (dc, ch 3, dc) in specified st or sp: V-st made.

Instructions

Ch 28.

Row 1 (wrong side): L-shell in 6th ch from hook, ch 7, skip next 7 chs, dc in next ch, ch 7, skip next 7 chs, L-shell in next ch, ch 7, skip next 5 chs, sc in last ch: 2 L-shells, 1 dc, 1 sc and 3 ch-7 sps; ch 3 (counts as dc on following row now and throughout), turn.

Row 2 (right side): Work 10 dc in first ch-7 sp, L-shell in ch-sp of L-shell, ch 5, skip next ch-7 sp, V-st in next dc, ch 5, skip next ch-7 sp, L-shell in ch-sp of L-shell, dc in top of turning ch: 2 L-shells, 1 V-st, 12 dc and 2 ch-5 sps; ch 3, turn.

Row 3: L-shell in ch-sp of L-shell, ch 4, 7 dc in ch-sp of V-st, ch 4, L-shell in ch-sp of L-shell, ch 1, dc in sp between first and 2nd dc of 10-dc group, (ch 1, dc in sp before next dc) 8 times, ch 1, dc in top of turning ch: 2 L-shells, 18 dc, 2 ch-4 sps and 10 ch-1 sps; ch 4 (counts as dc and ch-1 sp on following row), turn.

Row 4: (Dc in next ch-1 sp, ch 1) 10 times, L-shell in ch-sp of L-shell, ch 3, dc in sp between first and 2nd dc of 7-dc group, (ch 1, dc in sp before next dc) 5 times, ch 3, L-shell in ch-sp of L-shell, dc in top of turning ch: 2 L-shells, 18 dc, 2 ch-3 sps and 16 ch-1 sps; ch 3, turn.

Row 5: L-shell in ch-sp of L-shell, ch 3, 2 dc in each of next 5 ch-1 sps, ch 3, L-shell in ch-sp of L-shell, ch 2, (dc in next ch-1 sp, ch 2) 10 times, (dc, ch 2, dc) in turning ch-4 sp: 2 L-shells, 23 dc, 2 ch-3 sps and 12 ch-2 sps; ch 3, turn.

Row 6: S-shell in first ch-2 sp, skip next ch-2 sp, (S-shell in next ch-2 sp, skip next ch-2 sp) 5 times, L-shell in ch-sp of L-shell, ch 7, dc in sp between 5th and 6th dc of 10-dc group, ch 7, L-shell in ch-sp of L-shell, dc in top of turning ch: 2 L-shells, 6 S-shells, 3 dc and 2 ch-7 sps; ch 3, turn.

Row 7: L-shell in ch-sp of L-shell, ch 5, skip next ch-7 sp, V-st in next dc, ch 5, skip next ch-7 sp, L-shell in ch-sp of L-shell, S-shell in ch-sp of each of next 6 S-shells: 2 L-shells, 6 S-shells, 1 V-st, 1 dc and 2 ch-5 sps; ch 3, turn.

Row 8: S-shell in ch-sp of each of next 6 S-shells, ch 1, L-shell in ch-sp of L-shell, ch 4, 7 dc in ch-sp of V-st, ch 4, L-shell in ch-sp of L-shell, dc in top of turning ch: 2 L-shells, 6 S-shells, 9 dc, 2 ch-4 sps and 1 ch-1 sp; ch 3, turn.

Row 9: L-shell in ch-sp of L-shell, ch 3, dc in sp between first and 2nd dc of 7-dc group, (ch 1, dc in sp before next dc) 5 times, ch 3, L-shell in ch-sp of L-shell, ch 1, M-shell in ch-sp of each of next 6 S-shells: 2 L-shells, 6 M-shells, 7 dc, 2 ch-3 sps and 6 ch-1 sps; ch 3, turn.

Row 10: Work 10 dc in ch-sp of each of next 6 M-shells, ch 1, L-shell in ch-sp of L-shell, ch 3, 2 dc in each of next 5 ch-1 sps, ch 3, L-shell in ch-sp of L-shell, dc in top of turning ch: 2 L-shells, 71 dc, 2 ch-3 sps and 1 ch-1 sp; ch 3, turn.

Row 11: L-shell in ch-sp of L-shell, ch 7, dc in sp between 5th and 6th dc of 10-dc group, ch 7, L-shell in ch-sp of L-shell, ch 7, sc in sp between 5th and 6th dc of next 10-dc group: 2 L-shells, 2 dc, 1 sc and 3 ch-7 sps; ch 3, turn.

Rep Rows 2 through 11 for desired length, ending by working a Row 10 rep. Finish off; weave in ends.

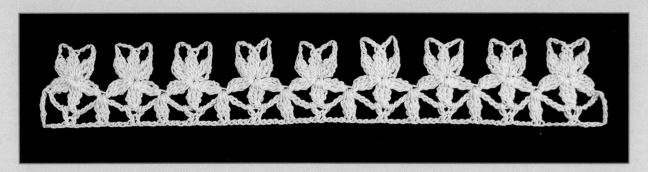

6-Petal Flowers

STITCH GUIDE

2-tr cl (2 triple crochet cluster): *YO twice, insert hook in specified st or sp and draw up a lp, (YO and draw through 2 lps on hook) twice; rep from * once; YO and draw through all 3 lps on hook: 2-tr cl made.

3-tr cl (3 triple crochet cluster): *YO twice, insert hook in specified st or sp and draw up a lp, (YO and draw through 2 lps on hook) twice; rep from * twice; YO and draw through all 4 lps on hook: 3-tr cl made.

Dc dec (double crochet decrease): YO, insert hook in first specified st or sp and draw up a lp, YO and draw through 2 lps on hook; YO, insert hook in 2nd specified st or sp and draw up a lp, YO and draw through 2 lps on hook; YO and draw through all 3 lps on hook: dc dec made.

Instructions

Row 1 (right side): *(Ch 5, 2-tr cl in 5th ch from hook) twice, (ch 5, 3-tr cl, ch 5, 2-tr cl, ch 4, sl st, ch 4, 2-tr cl) in same ch as last 2-tr cl (5 petals of flower made); rep from * across. Do not turn.

Row 2 (right side): Rotate piece to work along bottom edge of flowers; ch 5, 3-tr cl in same ch as last 2-tr cl (6th petal of flower made); *ch 5, sc in ch at base of first 2-tr cl on same flower**, ch 5, 3-tr cl in same ch as last 2-tr cl on next flower; rep from * across, ending last rep at **; ch 8 (counts as tr and ch-4 sp on following row), turn.

Row 3 (wrong side): Dc dec in first 2 ch-5 sps; *ch 4, 3-tr cl in same ch as next sc, ch 4, dc dec in next 2 ch-5 sps; rep from * across; ch 4, tr in top of last 2-tr cl on last flower. Finish off; weave in ends.

General Directions

Abbreviations and Symbols

Crochet patterns are written in a special shorthand which is used so that instructions don't take up too much space. They sometimes seem confusing, but once you learn them, you'll have no trouble following them.

These are Abbreviations

BB	Bobble		**FPtr**	front post triple crochet
BBcl	Bobble cluster		**Hdc**	half double crochet
Beg	beginning		**Inc**	Increase(ing)
BL	back loop		**Lp(s)**	loop(s)
BPc	back popcorn		**Patt**	pattern
BPdc	back post double crochet		**PC**	popcorn
BPsc	back post single crochet		**Prev**	previous
BPtr	back post triple crochet		**PS**	puff stitch
BS	basket stitch		**Rem**	remaining
Ch(s)	chain(s)		**Rep**	repeat(ing)
Cl(s)	cluster(s)		**Rnd(s)**	round(s)
Cont	continue		**Sc**	single crochet
Dc	double crochet		**Sc dec**	single crochet decrease
Dc Cl	double crochet cluster		**Sc2tog**	single crochet 2 stitches together
Dc dec	double crochet decrease		**SK**	skip
Dc inc	double crochet increase		**Sl st**	slip stitch
Dec	decrease		**Sp(s)**	space(s)
Dtr Cl	double triple crochet cluster		**St(s)**	stitch(es)
Dtr	double triple crochet		**Tog**	together
Fig	figure		**Tr**	triple crochet
FL	front loop		**V-st**	V-stitch
Fpc	front popcorn		**YO**	yarn over hook
FPdc	front post double crochet		**Y-st**	Y-stitch
FPsc	front post single crochet			

These are Standard Symbols

* An asterisk (or double asterisks**) in a pattern row, indicates a portion of instructions to be used more than once. For instance, "rep from * three times" means that after working the instructions once, you must work them again three times for a total of 4 times in all.

† A dagger (or double daggers ††) indicates that those instructions will be repeated again later in the same row or round.

: The number of stitches after a **colon** tells you the number of stitches you will have when you have completed the row or round.

( ) Parentheses enclose instructions which are to be worked the number of times following the parentheses. For instance, "(ch 1, sc, ch1) 3 times" means that you will chain one, work one sc, and then chain again three times for a total of six chains and three scs. Parentheses often set off or clarify a group of stitches to be worked into the same space or stitch. For instance, "(dc, ch2, dc) in corner sp."

[ ] Brackets and ( ) parentheses are also used to give you additional information.

Terms

Front Loop – This is the loop toward you at the top of the crochet stitch.

Back Loop – This is the loop away from you at the top of the crochet stitch.

Post – This is the vertical part of the crochet stitch.

Join – This means to join with a sl st unless another stitch is specified.

Finish Off – This means to end your piece by pulling the cut yarn end through the last loop remaining on the hook. This will prevent the work from unraveling.

The patterns in this book have been written using the crochet terminology that is used in the United States. Terms which may have different equivalents in other parts of the world are listed below.

United States	International
Double crochet (dc)	treble crochet (tr)
Gauge	tension
Half double crochet (hdc)	half treble crochet (htr)
Single crochet	double crochet
Skip	miss
Slip stitch	single crochet
Triple crochet (tr)	double treble crochet (dtr)
Yarn over (YO)	yarn forward (yfwd)

Standard Yarn Weights

To make it easier for yarn manufacturers, publishers, and designers to prepare consumer-friendly products and for consumers to select the right materials for a project, the following standard yarn weight system has been adopted.

Categories of yarn, gauge, ranges, and recommended hook sizes

Yarn Weight Symbol & Category Names	0 Lace	1 Super Fine	2 Fine	3 Light	4 Medium	5 Bulky	6 Super Bulky
Type of Yarns in Category	Fingering 10 count crochet	Sock Fingering, Baby	Sport, Baby	DK, Light, Worsted	Worsted, Afghan, Aran	Chunky, Craft, Rug	Bulky, Roving
Crochet Gauge* Ranges in Single Crochet to 4 inch	32-42 sts*	21-32 sts	16-20 sts	12-17 sts	11-14 sts	8-11 sts	5-9 sts
Recommended Hook in Metric Size Range	Steel** 1.6-1.4mm Regular Hook 2.25mm	2.25-3.5mm	3.5-4.5mm	4.5-5.5mm	5.5-6.5mm	6.5-9mm	9mm and larger
Recommended Hook in US Size Range	Steel** 6, 7, 8	B-1 to E-4	E-4 to 7	7 to I-9	I-9 to K-10.5	K-10.5 to M-13	M-13 and larger

*Lace weight yarns are usually crocheted on larger hooks to create lacy, openwork patterns. Accordingly, a gauge range is difficult to determine. Always follow the gauge stated in your pattern.
** Steel crochet hooks are sized differently from regular hooks—the higher the number, the smaller the hook, which is the reverse of regular hook sizing.

Skill Levels

Yarn manufacturers, publishers, needle and hook manufacturers have worked together to set up a series of guidelines and symbols to bring uniformity to patterns. Before beginning a project, check to see if your skill level is equal to the one listed for the project.

◖■☐☐◗	Beginner	Projects for first-time crocheters using basic stitches and minimal shaping.
◖■■☐◗	Easy	Projects using yarn with basic stitches, repetitive stitch patterns, simple color changes, and simple shaping and finishing.
◖■■■◗	Intermediate	Projects using a variety of techniques, such as basic lace patterns or color patterns, mid-level shaping and finishing.
◖■■■◗	Experienced	Projects with intricate stitch patterns, techniques and dimension, such as non-repeating patterns, multi-color techniques, fine threads, small hooks, detailed shaping and refined finishing.

Crochet Hooks

Thread crochet hooks are tiny hooks that are used to make very fine, lace weight projects, such as doilies and tablecloths. They are designed to be used with thinner threads than regular yarn crochet.

The hooks used most often for thread projects are about 5" long, which is shorter than most hooks used for yarns, and are constructed slightly differently. These hooks are made from steel which is a harder metal than those used in yarn hooks and is less liable to break at the hook end. This end can be very narrow on the smallest steel hooks. Some steel hooks come with a plastic handle—or you can purchase a rubber handle to place over your steel hook—to make the grip more comfortable, especially when crocheting for long periods of time.

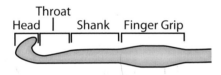

The hook end is a little sharper than found on yarn hooks; then comes the throat, which gradually becomes thicker until it forms the shank, the area on which the stitches must be formed. Then the hook thickens again until it reaches the finger grip. It is important that every stitch be made on the shank, not on the throat (which will cause the stitches to be too tight) or on the area beyond the shank (which will cause the stitches to be too loose).

Steel thread crochet hooks are sized differently from regular yarn hooks. In fact the sizing is the exact opposite. The higher the number, the smaller the hook, which is the reverse of yarn hook sizing. Steel thread crochet hooks sold by American manufacturers range in size from 14 (the finest) to 00 (the thickest). Even finer hooks are sold in other countries where much more delicate lace work is often created.

Different countries actually use different numbering systems. Here is a chart which can help clear up any confusion. It shows hook sizes in both the US and the UK.

Steel Hook Conversion Chart

Metric	US	UK/Canadian
3.5 mm	00	—
3.25 mm	0	0
2.75 mm	1	1
2.25 mm	2	$1^1/_2$
2.1 mm	3	2
2.0 mm	4	$2^1/_2$
1.9 mm	5	3
1.8 mm	6	$3^1/_2$
1.65 mm	7	4
1.5 mm	8	$4^1/_2$
1.4 mm	9	5
1.3 mm	10	$5^1/_2$
1.1 mm	11	6
1.0 mm	12	$6^1/_2$
.85 mm	13	7
.75 mm	14	—

Crochet Thread

The thread used for thread crochet comes in a number of sizes ranging from a very thin size 100 to a thick size 5. The larger the number, the finer the thread. Size 10, commonly called bedspread weight, is the thread most commonly used (and the one that is used for most of the projects in this book).

Crochet thread is produced by various manufacturers and sold under a number of brand names. The labels on the thread will tell you how much thread in ounces, grams, meters and yards is in the ball. It will also tell you about the fiber content of the thread—usually cotton—and its washability. The label will also give you the dye lot number of the particular ball or skein. The same color—even white or ecru—can vary from dye lot to dye lot. Make certain that all of the thread used for a project is from the same dye lot. Otherwise you may notice variations in color when the project is completed.

Working Into the Starting Chains

When working the first row of stitches into a starting chain, you will always need to skip one or more chain stitches first, depending on how tall the new stitch will be. You can never work into the very first chain from the hook, as it will unravel.

To work a stitch into the chain, insert the hook from the front of the chain through the center of a V stitch and under the corresponding bump on the back of the same stitch.

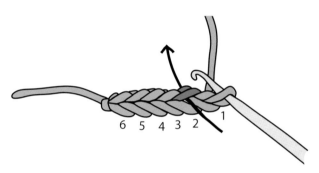

Not including the first stitch, work into every stitch in the chain (unless the pattern tells you to work differently), but not into the beginning slip knot. Make certain that you work the last chain at the end of the row.

Unless otherwise specified in the instructions, use the following:

For sc: Work in the 2nd ch from the hook. The skipped chains do not count as a stitch. Make one more chain than the final number of stitches needed.

For hdc: Work in the 3rd chain from the hook. The skipped chains count as a stitch. Make two more chains than the final number of stitches needed.

For dc: Work in the 4th chain from the hook. The skipped chains count as a stitch. Make two more chains than the final number of stitches needed.

For tr: Work in the 5th chain from the hook. The skipped chains count as a stitch. Make three more chains than the final number of stitches needed.

Turning Chains

To work another row of single crochet stitches, you will need to turn the piece and work back into the single crochet stitches just made. Whenever you turn the work to start a new row, you will need to first work one or more chain stitches to bring the thread up to the height of the next row. This is called the "turning chain." For single crochet you will need to work only one chain, then turn the chain in the direction of the arrow (counterclockwise) as shown below.

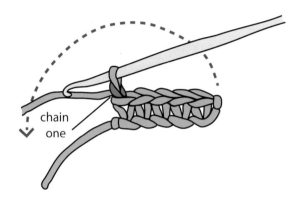

chain one

Unless otherwise specified in the instructions, use the following:

For sc: One turning chain; it does not count as a stitch on the following row so the next stitch is worked into the very first stitch of the following row.

For hdc: Two turning chains; the chains count as the first stitch of the following row, so the first stitch is skipped and the next hdc is worked in the second stitch.

For dc: Three turning chains; the chains count as the first stitch of the following row. The first stitch is therefore skipped and the next dc is worked in the second stitch.

For tr: Four turning chains; the chains count as the first stitch of the following row, so the first stitch is skipped and the next tr is worked in the second stitch.

Finishing a Project

After you have completed your project, you will need to weave in all thread ends.

A size 18 steel tapestry needle, which is a blunt-pointed sewing needle with an eye big enough to carry the thread as you weave in ends, is necessary for securely weaving in all thread ends.

Thread the tapestry needle with the thread, and weave the running stitches either horizontally or vertically on the wrong side of the work. Start by weaving about 1" in one direction and then ½" in the opposite direction. Make certain that the thread does not show on the right side of the work. Cut off excess thread.

Washing

Despite the fragile appearance of threadwork, it is very durable and can last a lifetime with proper care. Always wash the item when you finish crocheting it. The thread undergoes a lot of handling during construction and the oils from your hands can soil the work. Washing and blocking helps to "set" the stitches resulting in a neat and uniform appearance and giving your work a "professional" look.

Using a mild detergent and warm water (never hot!), gently squeeze suds through the piece. Being careful not to rub, twist or wring, rinse the piece several times in cool, clear water. Roll it in an absorbent towel and gently press out the excess moisture.

Blocking

After washing the design and while it is still wet, place it on a blocking board, an ironing board, or a piece of cardboard covered with a towel. Pin the design to shape with rustproof pins, making sure that all of the stitches and rows in the design are straight. Allow the design to dry completely.

Project Notes

If you are crocheting an edging for a project that you will be making in multiples, such as pillowcases or curtains, you may want to photocopy this page to create a record of your project details for later use.

Edging title and page reference:_____

Chain multiple, if any:_____

Length made:_____ Count for starting chain:_____

Notes: _____

_____

Edging title and page reference:_____

Chain multiple, if any:_____

Length made:_____ Count for starting chain:_____

Notes: _____

_____

Edging title and page reference:_____

Chain multiple, if any:_____

Length made:_____ Count for starting chain:_____

Notes: _____

_____

Edging title and page reference:_____

Chain multiple, if any:_____

Length made:_____ Count for starting chain:_____

Notes: _____

_____

Key to Edgings on Front Cover

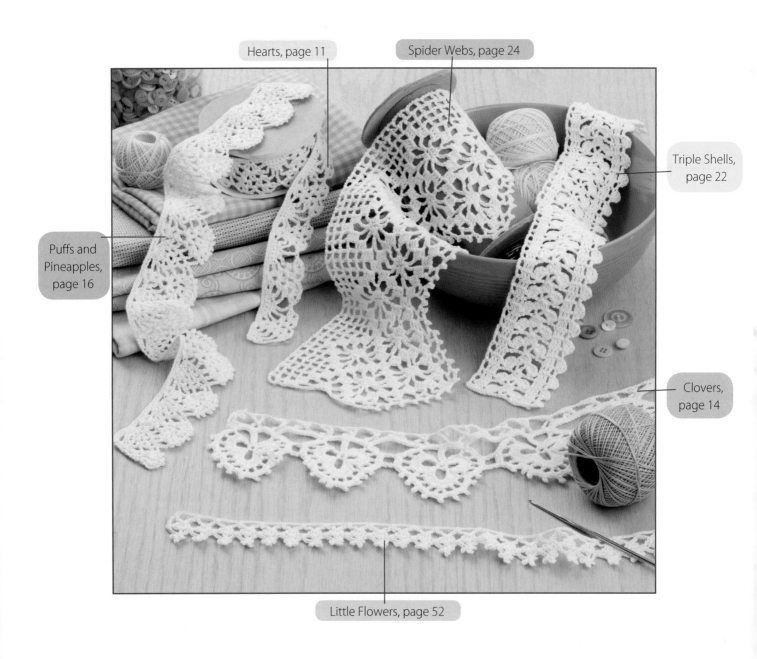

Hearts, page 11

Spider Webs, page 24

Triple Shells, page 22

Puffs and Pineapples, page 16

Clovers, page 14

Little Flowers, page 52

Thread Information

The edgings shown on the Front Cover were made using Aunt Lydia's® Classic™ Size 10 Crochet Thread (Article 154) in color #0001 White.

Photography models for the Front Cover were made by Marianna Crowder.

CONTRIBUTORS:

Mike Grove
Don Logan
Dave Ostrowski
Kevin Suddarth
Carlo Tripodi
Bob Stewart
Bill Sides
Brian Pickering

Lindsay Peacock
Mike Campbell
Pete Berganini
Brian Rogers
Bill Spidle
Jerry Geer
Phillip Huston
Jim Rotramel

Jim Leslie
Don Spering/A.I.R.
Flightleader
Picciani Aircraft Slides
Military Aircraft Photographs
Centurion Enterprises
GB Aircraft Slides
U.S. Navy

FIRST EDITION
FIRST PRINTING

Published in United States by

TAB BOOKS
Blue Ridge Summit, PA 17294-0214

Library of Congress Cataloging
in Publication Data

Kinzey, Bert.
U.S. Navy F-4 Phantoms / by Bert Kinzey and Ray Leader.
p. cm. — (Colors and markings : v. 17-)
Includes index.
Contents: Pt. 1. Atlantic coast markings
ISBN 0-8306-4541-1 (pbk)
1. Phantom II (Jet fighter plane) 2. Airplanes, Military—United States—Identification marks. 3. United States. Navy—Aviation. I. Leader, Ray. II. Title. III. Title: US Navy F-4 Phantoms.
IV. Series: C&M ; vol. 17, etc.
UG1242.F5K5484   1991
359.9′4834′0973—dc20   90-11314
                                          CIP

First published in Great Britain in 1991
by Airlife Publishing Ltd.
7 St. John's Hill, Shrewsbury, SY1 1JE

British Library Cataloging In
Publication Data

Kinzey, Bert 1945-
U.S. Navy F-4 Phantoms.
1. McDonnell Douglas F-4 aeroplanes, history
I. Title II. Leader, Ray III. Series
623.7464

ISBN 1-85310-624-0

Questions regarding the content of this book
should be addressed to:

Reader Inquiry Branch
TAB BOOKS Inc.
Blue Ridge Summit, PA 17294-0214

Front cover: An F-4J from VF-33 and the USS AMERICA heads inbound on a mission over North Vietnam. Note that the aircraft is armed with both air-to-air and air-to-ground ordnance. Triple ejector racks under each of the inner wing pylons carry 500-pound Snakeeye high-drag bombs, and Sidewinder missiles are shoulder mounted on the same pylons. A 600-gallon fuel tank is carried on the centerline station. It is interesting to note that the retractable boarding ladder is extended.
(U.S. Navy)

Rear cover top: This air-to-air photograph shows one of VF-11's Phantoms in the early colorful markings and the light gull gray over white scheme. The Red Rippers were assigned to the air wing aboard the USS FORRESTAL when this photograph was taken.
(U.S. Navy)

Rear cover bottom: This view of an F-4S from VF-201 illustrates one of the few Phantoms to serve in the "official" tactical scheme designed for the F-4 late in its operational life. It provides a nice contrast with the colorful scheme and markings shown in the top photo. The aircraft was photographed as it began to taxi out for a training flight to the bombing range.
(Grove)

COLORS & MARKINGS
OF

U.S. Navy
F-4 Phantoms

Bert Kinzey and Ray Leader

TAB BOOKS
Blue Ridge Summit, PA

Airlife Publishing Ltd.

England

INTRODUCTION

*The first official paint scheme used on Navy Phantoms is illustrated in this photograph of an F-4J from VF-33. This is the light gull gray over white scheme, and the unit's markings are large and colorful. In this case the entire vertical fin and rudder are painted black. The **AG** tail code is located within a yellow star and lightning bolt. **VF-33** is lettered boldly on the upper fuselage, and the carrier name, **USS INDEPENDENCE,** is above **NAVY** on the aft fuselage. Markings such as these were typical of those used by most Phantom squadrons until the low visibility and tactical schemes began to appear in the late 1970s.* (Flightleader)

On December 17, 1903, the Wright brothers made the first powered flight by an aircraft that was heavier than air, and aviation as we know it today was born. To most people alive today, aircraft are so commonplace that the thought of a world without them is incomprehensible. But there are also people alive today who were living when Orville and Wilbur Wright wrote that first page in the history of modern aviation. In all of the pages that have followed, there have been many dramatic and unbelievable feats accomplished. The technology that began with motorized box kites produced aircraft that flew faster and faster and higher and higher. Man developed aircraft that shattered the sound barrier, then doubled and tripled the speed of sound in short order. He proved that the phrase "the sky's the limit" was not true for aviators as he stepped onto the surface of the moon and brought back pieces of its crust. But there are two related facts that are the most unbelievable of all others relating to modern aviation. First, of the many thousands of years that man has walked this earth, powered, heavier-than-air machines have flown for less than one hundred years --an almost infinitesimally small segment of the overall

history of man. Second, all of the remarkable advances in aviation, from the Wright Flyer to the SR-71, the stealth aircraft, and the space shuttle, have occurred within a single lifetime.

During this short period of time, hundreds and hundreds of different aircraft have been built. Many were failures or disappointments, and relatively few were the true successes that their designers hoped they would be. Still fewer have become classics that have left an indelible mark in the pages of aviation history. Among those classics are the Ford Tri-Motor, the DC-3, the Me-109, the Spitfire, and the P-51 Mustang. Among jet-powered aircraft, the F-86 can be counted as a classic, but it is the F-4 Phantom that would top the list of most aviation historians and enthusiasts in the free world. Designed originally as a fleet defense fighter for the U.S. Navy, the F-4 Phantom went on to prove its versatility in a number of other roles while serving with the Navy, the Marines, the U.S. Air Force, and in the air forces of several other nations around the world. Phantoms are still in service today, and have been in the skies for well over one third of the entire time since the Wright brothers visited the

Still carrying colorful markings, this F-4N is painted in the overall light gull gray scheme. When applied to other types of aircraft, this scheme was usually seen with low-visibility markings of black and grays with little, if any, color.

windy beaches of North Carolina. It is no wonder that the Phantom is one of the most popular aircraft in the history of aviation.

Perhaps it is because the Navy had the F-4 Phantom designed and built, and was the first service to use it operationally, or perhaps it is because Navy Phantoms usually carried the most colorful markings of any F-4s that ever flew, but it seems that the Navy's Phantoms are the most popular and best loved and remembered by the enthusiasts today. Compared to the drab camouflaged Phantoms flown by the Air Force and by most foreign countries, Navy Phantoms seemed to be the more exciting and flashier aircraft. While the beauty and the color was only skin deep, its appeal to the eye, the camera, and the enthusiast is undeniable.

These F-4 Phantoms of the U.S. Navy will be covered in two parts in the Colors & Markings Series. In this book, all squadrons that have carried markings of the Atlantic Fleet and are shore-based on the Atlantic coast are illustrated. These include all of the fighter squadrons that operated the Phantom with the Atlantic Fleet as well as the reserve squadrons assigned to the Atlantic Fleet. Since it is the markings of the Atlantic Fleet that are covered, rather than the squadrons themselves, three Pacific Fleet squadrons, VF-142, VF-143, and VF-151 are

also included. For a time, these squadrons operated aboard aircraft carriers of the Atlantic Fleet, and their aircraft are illustrated during these deployments to the Atlantic and the Mediterranean Sea. Additionally, test and evaluation units based on or near the east coast are covered. Markings for the Blue Angels' F-4J Phantoms are shown as well. In all, twenty-two different units are illustrated. Part two of our coverage of the markings applied to Navy F-4s will be released in about a year, and will include all Pacific Fleet squadrons, Pacific reserve squadrons, and the test and evaluation units located in the western United States. Together, these two volumes in the Colors & Markings Series will provide the most extensive coverage ever published on the markings carried by the Navy's Phantoms.

When the Phantom entered service with the Navy, the official paint scheme prescribed for Navy fighters consisted of light gull gray (FS 36440) upper surfaces and white under surfaces. White was also applied to the rudder and the tops of the flaps, ailerons, and the outer portions of the horizontal stabilizers. Wheel wells, struts, and wheels were also white, as were the interiors of the air intakes. Colorful unit markings were applied to the vertical tail surfaces, the fuselage, and the nose of the aircraft.

*The tactical scheme has been applied to this F-4S from VF-103. Although a little color remains in the form of a thin yellow outline of an arrow on the tail, most other markings are subdued grays. The **211** on the nose, the **11** on the fin cap, and the names on the canopy rails are gloss black.*

(Grove)

These colorful markings on the light gull gray over white scheme remained the norm throughout almost all of the Phantom's operational life with the Navy. Indeed, the Phantom's replacement, the F-14 Tomcat, entered service in this scheme, and remained in it for a number of years. As the move to lower visibility schemes and markings began, the overall light gull gray scheme was used on the Navy's Phantoms with both colorful and subdued markings. Even a few Phantoms remained in Navy squadrons long enough to see the first of the tactical schemes and markings. These colorless schemes were the result of attempts to reduce the visual and infrared signatures of the aircraft.

Because the low visibility and tactical schemes were so short lived before the F-4 was phased out of service with the Navy, there seems to be little if any in the way of official direction. If there was any, it certainly was not followed very diligently by the units. In the last few years of their operational service with the Navy, Phantoms could be seen in overall light gull gray with black or gray markings, in various other shades of gray, both permanently and temporarily applied, and in several variations of the tactical scheme. Almost all color disappeared, and the once attractive fighters looked dull and uninspiring.

Because Navy Phantoms carried the bright colors throughout most of their service, the majority of the photographs in this book illustrate the extensive and bright colors applied by the various squadrons. But we have also included photographs that illustrate the low visibility and tactical schemes and markings. We have chosen the photographs for this publication, not to provide a pretty picture book, but to illustrate both dramatic and subtle changes in markings, and to make the coverage as complete as possible. Regular fleet squadrons are illustrated first, and are presented in numerical order. These are followed by the reserve squadrons, which are also arranged in numerical order, then the test and evaluation units and the Blue Angels conclude the coverage. Many contributors helped make this book as complete as possible. Their names are listed on page two, and the authors would like to thank them and acknowledge their assistance.

The Phantom will always remain a classic and a favorite among historians and the fans of aircraft and aviation in general. But none of the units illustrated in this book fly the Phantom any longer. It has been replaced by newer aircraft, or the squadrons have been disestablished. Our hope is that this book, and the forthcoming second part, will provide an important and worthwhile record of these squadrons and their markings when they flew one of the truly classic aircraft in aviation history-- the F-4 Phantom.

VF-11 RED RIPPERS

An excellent example of colorful markings can be seen here on F-4B, 152965. The photograph was taken in May 1973 while the aircraft was assigned to VF-11 and painted in CAG markings. *(Picciani Aircraft Slides)*

At left is an overall view of F-4B, 152307, which was also painted in very colorful markings for VF-11. Notice the red lightning bolt on the travel pod under the wing. At right is a close-up of the tail that provides a good look at the squadron badge. *(Both Flightleader Collection)*

F-4B, 153052, was also assigned to the Red Rippers during the same time period. This aircraft did not have the squadron badge applied to the tail as seen above. *(Flightleader)*

*A change in markings for VF-11 is illustrated in the photograph at left, which was taken in November 1974. By this time the squadron had already transitioned to F-4Js. At right is a close-up of the revised markings. Notice the much larger squadron badge and boar's head than shown on the previous page. The **AA** tail codes were black, shadowed in white, and the lightning bolt was red.*
(Both Flightleader)

During America's Bi-centennial celebration, VF-11 added red, white, and blue stripes to the fin cap and wing tips on their aircraft. Notice the colorful CAG markings applied to the white rudder. *(Logan)*

*F-4J, 157291, had a smaller squadron badge applied to the bottom of the splitter plate. An award for excellence was represented by a large **E** which was painted in red and shadowed with white. It can be seen at the top of the plate.* *(Ostrowski)*

Special Bi-centennial markings had been applied to the fuselage of F-4J, 157276. The red, white, and blue **76** was surrounded by stars, and had **FIGHTING FOR FREEDOM** lettered in black around it.　　　　*(Flightleader)*

F-4J, 157308, was the CAG aircraft for the Red Rippers when this photograph was taken on April 29, 1977. A vertical row of bars was painted on the white rudder.　　　*(Flightleader)*

VF-11 had started to tone down their markings by November 1979. This overall gray Phantom still carried some color in its markings, but the white shadowing had disappeared from the **AA** tail codes and the **VF-11.**
　　　　　　　　　　(Grove)

VF-14 TOP HATTERS

F-4B, 149417, was assigned to VF-14 when this photograph was taken in 1966. The red chevron on the fuselage contained a black top hat on a white disc. The fin cap was red, and the **AB** tail codes were black. (MAP)

Another VF-14 "B" Phantom is seen in this photograph taken in 1973, and a slight change can be seen in the markings on the tail. The black **AB** tail codes were shadowed with red. (Flightleader)

A different style of tail codes is illustrated in this photograph of F-4B, 150450, which was taken on July 20, 1968. The red chevron and top hat emblem had been moved to the tail. (Picciani Aircraft Slides)

Another variation of markings for the Top Hatters is shown in this view of F-4B, 151430. A red chevron was painted on the tail along with the **AB** tail codes, which were black and outlined in red. **VF-14** was lettered in red on the white centerline tank. (Picciani Aircraft Slides)

VF-31 TOMCATTERS

*ither colorful squadron in the early 1970s was VF-31. This F-4J, 157308, was painted in full markings, and was tographed at NAS Miramar, California. The red horizontal stripes on the tail contained the black **AC** tail codes which e shadowed in white.*
(Flightleader Collection)

*Another Phantom from VF-31 was photographed on the deck of the USS SARATOGA, and was painted in colorful markings. The red checkmark along the side of the fuselage had **VF-31** painted in black which was shadowed with white. The squadron emblem on the fuselage was painted black and white on a yellow disc.*
(Flightleader Collection)

 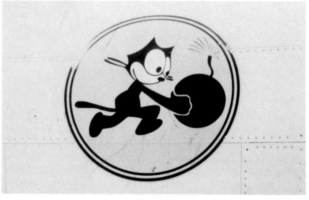

At left is an overall view of F-4J, 155848. At right is a close-up view of the squadron badge that was painted on the fuse-lage.
(Left Logan, right Flightleader)

10

For a short time, VF-31 had individual nose art and names painted inside the nose wheel door of several of their aircraft. At left is an overall view of an aircraft marked in this manner. At right is a close-up view of the Spook and the name **MIG EATER,** both of which were painted in black and red. (Both Centurion Enterprises)

This Phantom carried the **100** modex for the CAG aircraft, even though no other special markings were present. (Flightleader)

This left front view of F-4J, 153809, was taken on the deck of the USS SARATOGA. The centerline tank had a black Felix the Cat figure, with **1776-1976** painted above it in red, white, and blue for the Bi-centennial celebration. (Tripodi)

This CAG aircraft for VF-31 was photographed in the landing pattern on April 19, 1977. It did not have any special markings for the CAG other than the **100** modex, and was painted in the gray over white scheme.

(Flightleader)

F-4J, 155861, from VF-31, had the carrier name **USS SARATOGA** positioned under the red bands on the tail. This was different from the location seen in the photograph at the top of this page. This Phantom was painted in the overall gloss gray scheme.

(Ostrowski)

This F-4J was also a CAG aircraft for VF-31. The colorful checkmarks on the rudder were a different approach to CAG markings than previously used by this unit.

(Ostrowski)

VF-32 SWORDSMEN

F-4B, 149431, was assigned to VF-32 when this photograph was taken on July 10, 1968. The sword on the fuselage was painted yellow, and had a black handle. **VF-32** was lettered in black, and the wing tips and the fin cap were yellow. The banner under the tail codes was black and white.

(Picciani Aircraft Slides)

A variation to VF-32's markings is illustrated by this view of F-4B, 152290. The **AB** tail codes on the tail were slanted instead of being horizontal. A sword had been painted vertically on the rudder, and the chevron on the tail was black and yellow.

(Picciani Aircraft Slides)

The same style of markings as shown in the photograph above was also used on F-4B, 152226. This photograph is dated July 15, 1971.

(Flightleader Collection)

The Swordsmen's CAG aircraft was very colorful on August 5, 1970, when this photograph was taken. Notice the multi-colored diamonds painted on the blade of the sword. These were the markings for the CAG. One could only wish that their F-14s carried such beautiful markings!

(Picciani Aircraft Slides)

13

VF-33 TARSIERS

The markings used on VF-33's F-4Bs during the late 1960s were very attractive. The yellow rudder had black stars arranged vertically. **VF-33-USS AMERICA** was painted in black along the bottom of the tail. The aircraft illustrated on the front cover is also painted in this scheme.

(MAP)

A slight variation in the Tarsiers' markings is shown on F-4B, 152306, which was photographed in August 1966. **VF-33** had been removed from the tail, and was relocated above the yellow lightning bolt on the fuselage. The **AE** tail codes were black, edged with yellow.

(Picciani Aircraft Slides)

VF-33 had changed their markings by the time this photograph was taken in 1971. Notice the change in tail codes from **AE** to **AG**. These codes were black on a yellow disc. The lightning bolt on the fuselage and the stripe up the front of the tail were painted yellow and edged in black. A small black lightning bolt and **VF-33** were painted on the yellow rudder. (Flightleader)

The Tarsiers had transitioned into F-4Js and changed their markings by the time this photograph was taken in October 1973. A change in carrier assignments is indicated by the **USS INDEPENDENCE** stencilled in black along the bottom of the tail. The **AG** tail codes were black on a yellow star, and the star was outlined in black. The leading edge and fin cap on the tail and down the rudder was yellow. There was a black and red MiG kill marking painted on the bottom of the splitter plate.

(Centurion Enterprises)

At left is an overall view of F-4J, 155747, which illustrates another change in markings for VF-33. The black color extends from the nose, beneath the canopy, along the spine of the fuselage, and across the entire tail. At right is a close-up view of the markings on the tail.

(Both Flightleader)

This view of F-4J, 155902, was taken on the deck of the USS INDEPENDENCE on February 11, 1976. It shows that the black had disappeared from the spine of the aircraft by this time.

(Tripodi)

F-4J, 155592, is shown here as it appeared on May 5, 1978. Note that the aircraft had the in-flight refueling probe extended. The **201** modex on the nose and **VF-33** on the fuselage were painted in black, shadowed with yellow.   (Kinzey)

Another of VF-33's Phantoms was photographed while in the landing pattern on April 29, 1977. This aircraft was painted in the overall gray scheme.   (Flightleader)

A change in carrier assignments had taken place by the time this photograph of F-4J, 155532, was taken in May 1978. The name **USS DWIGHT D EISENHOWER** was lettered in yellow on the bottom of the black tail. **CVW-7** was painted on the middle of the rudder, and colored stars were arranged vertically for the CAG markings.

(Flightleader Collection)

By October 14, 1978, the Tarsiers had been reassigned back to the USS INDEPENDENCE. This Phantom was painted overall gloss gray with a black *AE* tail code on the yellow star. Noticeable by its absence was all the black paint formerly on the nose and tail of the aircraft. *(Ostrowski)*

This Phantom was also painted in the overall gray scheme and was photographed on April 28, 1979. Notice the extended ram air turbine. *(Flightleader)*

VF-33 had started to tone down their markings by the time this photograph was taken on May 3, 1980. Notice the smaller gray stars and bars on this aircraft. *(Flightleader)*

17

VF-41 BLACK ACES

F-4J, 154783, was one of VF-41's Phantoms, and was painted in their full markings. The red stripe, positioned diagonally across the tail, was outlined with a black border, and it contained white stars that got smaller in size from bottom to top. The **AE** tail codes were white on the black spade. *(Flightleader)*

A pair of VF-41's aircraft are seen here while on short final in 1971. Notice the difference in the rudders of these two aircraft. One has the stars, and the other does not. The white stars in the red tail band, seen in the photograph above, were missing on both of these aircraft. *(Picciani Aircraft Slides)*

F-4J, 155746, was photographed on the deck of the USS FRANKLIN D. ROOSEVELT. This aircraft had the black stars on the rudder.

(Suddarth)

The Black Aces had transitioned back to F-4Bs from the "J" model by the time this photograph was taken on April 16, 1974. This was because the flying characteristics of the older variant were better suited to the smaller MIDWAY class carriers. The same markings used on the F-4Js were used on this F-4B. (Picciani Aircraft Slides)

This view illustrates the markings applied to the right side of the aircraft. (Flightleader)

VF-41's F-4Bs had been converted to F-4Ns by the time 152272 was photographed on March 8, 1974. The markings had not been changed except for the deletion of the small black stars that had been previously painted on the rudder. Notice the small squadron badge on the small travel pod.

(Flightleader Collection)

VF-41's CAG aircraft had small stars of various colors painted vertically on the white rudder. It doesn't show well in this view, but the rank of the flight crew was painted in blue and gold at the leading edge of the rectangle that contained their name. These rectangles or bands can be seen on the canopy rails.   (Centurion Enterprises)

At left is the right side of F-4N, 150632, which was photographed at Dobbins AFB, Georgia, on November 21, 1975. At right is a close-up view of the Bi-centennial markings painted in red, white, and blue on the tail.(Both Flightleader)

The Black Aces' markings are clearly illustrated in this photograph that was taken as the aircraft made its final approach to landing.
                (Picciani Aircraft Slides)

VF-74 BEDEVILERS

F-4B, 153047, was painted in the markings of VF-74 when this photograph was taken. The **AA** tail codes were white, shadowed with black, and had a red lightning bolt running through them. The carrier name **USS FORRESTAL** was in black along the bottom of the tail.

(Flightleader Collection)

This view of the left side of F-4B, 150422, shows the markings on that side of the aircraft. Notice that the carrier's name is missing from this Phantom. *(Flightleader Collection)*

*A change in the tail codes is evident in this photograph of F-4B, 150479. The **AJ** on the tail was black and the lightning bolt was red. No special CAG markings were on this aircraft, except for the **100** modex on the nose. (Flightleader)*

21

This photograph of F-4J, 153835, was taken in early 1973, and it illustrates some of the more colorful markings used on Phantoms. VF-74's markings during this time period made interesting subjects for photographers. The carrier name **USS AMERICA** was lettered in black on the rear of the fuselage.

(Ostrowski)

The opposite side of the same aircraft is shown here. It is interesting to see how the stripes on the fuselage and tail were extended onto the rudder.

(Flightleader)

VF-74's markings had been changed by the time this photograph was taken on April 5, 1975. The carrier name **USS FORRESTAL** on the fuselage and the **AA** tail codes indicated a change in carrier assignments.   (Flightleader)

By April 1977, VF-74 had been reassigned to the USS NIMITZ. This aircraft displays different markings that date from the Bi-centennial period. The **AJ** tail codes were again in use, and the squadron emblem was painted in black on the tail.   (Kinzey)

At left is a close-up view of the red, white, and blue Bi-centennial markings on the right side of the tail of 155824. At right is the opposite side of the tail.
          (Both Kinzey)

After serving aboard the USS NIMITZ, VF-74 was reassigned to the USS FORRESTAL. The carrier name and the **AA** tail codes were both painted white. This aircraft was painted in the overall gloss gray scheme.
(Flightleader Collection)

As VF-74 changed to low visibility markings, some of the color was replaced with dark gray as illustrated here. This aircraft still retained the white **AA** tail codes and **211** modex, as well as the yellow lightning bolt on the tail.
(Grove)

An interesting comparison is seen in this photograph which is dated October 10, 1981. The lightning bolt on the tail of the aircraft to the left was painted yellow while the one on 155881 was red. All other markings on this aircraft were dark gray.
(Ostrowski)

This CAG aircraft did not carry any special markings except for the **200** modex. All markings were black except for the yellow lightning bolt on the tail.
(Stewart)

The tactical paint scheme had made its appearance with VF-74 by the time this photograph was taken in February 1982. Notice that the red lightning bolt was painted on the front of the tail and not through the tail codes. (Grove)

F-4J, 153908, displays the markings painted on the right side of the aircraft. For tactical schemes, this one was rather attractive! (Grove)

In 1981, VF-74 painted F-4J, 153777, in special markings to commemorate their milestone of spending twenty years in Phantoms. At left is an overall view of this aircraft. At right is a close-up view of the markings painted on the tail. Modelers should note that 1/48th scale decals for this interesting aircraft are available from Detail & Scale on sheet number DS-06-48. (Both Ostrowski)

VF-84 JOLLY ROGERS

F-4J, 155861, exhibits some of the colorful markings used by the Jolly Rogers of VF-84. The white skull and crossed bones, the **AE** tail codes, and **5861** were all arranged on the solid black vertical tail. Small white stars were positioned vertically on the rudder, and the fin cap was painted yellow. The fuselage band was black, edged with yellow, and contained yellow chevrons.

(Flightleader)

This left front view shows the markings on another of VF-84's Phantoms. Notice the small skull and crossed bones and the black and yellow band on the travel pod.

(Flightleader)

This aircraft from VF-84 was photographed while it was "dirtied up" for landing in late 1971.

(Picciani Aircraft Slides)

The right side of this aircraft displays more of the markings used by the Jolly Rogers. The squadron was operating the F-4N version of the Phantom at this time.

(Centurion Enterprises)

The carrier name **USS ROOSEVELT** was lettered in black on the upper fuselage of this aircraft. This Phantom was photographed while on static display at an open house at NAS Oceana, Virginia, on August 16, 1975.

(Flightleader)

At left is a close-up view of the fuselage band on this aircraft. At right is a close-up look at the markings on the tail.

(Both Flightleader)

VF-101 GRIM REAPERS

This photograph of F-4A, 145307, shows the markings that were painted on the aircraft for project "Sageburner". The squadron designation **VF 101 DET A** was in black on the rear of the fuselage. *(Picciani Aircraft Slides)*

A later F-4A from VF-101 was photographed in 1965. The aircraft was painted in the gray over white scheme, and the **AD** tail codes were black.

(MAP)

Some rather unusual commander's markings were painted on F-4B, 152303. The horizontal stripes on the white rudder were red. The red fin cap contained the modex **000** in white, and this was repeated in black on the nose. The name **CAPT KNUTSON** was lettered in black on the bottom of the front canopy rail.

(Flightleader Collection)

28

F-4B, 151431, shows some slightly different markings used by VF-101. The small black chevron on the tail was shadowed with white as was the **AD** tail code. *(Flightleader Collection)*

These rather colorful CAG markings appeared on F-4J, 153769. The multicolored bands on the white rudder designated the CAG aircraft. **COMMANDER ATTACK CARRIER WING FOUR** was stencilled in black across the fuselage. The aircraft had probably been assigned to VF-101 only a short time before this photograph had been taken, and had only the **AD** tail code for its unit markings.
(Flightleader Collection)

This Phantom had the squadron badge painted on the splitter plate and red horizontal stripes on the rudder. The red fin cap contained the **110** modex in white. *(Flightleader)*

F-4J, 153777, was assigned to VF-101, Det-D, as indicated by the black lettering on the upper fuselage.
(Flightleader Collection)

Another aircraft assigned to VF-101, Det-D, is shown in this photograph, which illustrates the markings on the left side of 153826. The fin cap was red. (Flightleader Collection)

A slight change in markings for VF-101 is seen in this photograph of 153899. Notice that a red stripe had been painted up the leading edge of the vertical tail and across the fin cap. (Flightleader)

The Grim Reapers had made a minor alteration to their markings by the time this Phantom was photographed on December 14, 1974. The slanted **AD** tail codes were painted in black and were shadowed with white. A large squadron badge had been applied to the fuselage. (Flightleader)

At left is a close-up view of the red and white squadron badge used by VF-101 at that time. At right is a view of the splitter plate on another one of the squadron's aircraft which carried a smaller squadron badge painted in white on a dark red disc. (Both Flightleader)

VF-101 had some of the more colorful Bi-centennial markings used in the Navy. The entire tail was painted red, white, and blue and the **AD** tail code was in black that was shadowed in gold. The inscription **1776 - 1976** was lettered in gold in the blue portion of the tail.

(Kinzey)

F-4J, 153892, displays the colorful markings painted on the right side of the aircraft. *(Flightleader)*

The F-4B seen in this photograph was an O-J-T aircraft used for maintenance training by VF-101. The aircraft had a variation from the usual Bi-centennial markings used by this squadron. Red, white, and blue stripes were painted up the leading edge of the tail, and **1776 - 1976** was lettered in red and blue at the bottom of the tail.
(Centurion Enterprises)

VF-101 (KEY WEST DETACHMENT)

Colorful markings were also used on the Phantoms flown by VF-101's Key West detachment. This detachment provided ACM (Air Combat Maneuvering) training at NAS Key West, Florida, for east coast squadrons.   (Flightleader)

VF-101KW detachment had nice Bi-centennial markings applied to its air-craft. This F-4N had red, white, and blue chevrons on the tail of the aircraft and red stars positioned vertically on the rudder.   (Logan)

At left is a closer look at the squadron emblem on the fuselage, which was red, white, and blue. At right is a close-up view of the markings on the right side of the fuselage.
          (Both Sides)

VF-102 DIAMONDBACKS

F-4B, 151401, was assigned to VF-102, and displays some of the Diamondbacks' earlier markings. The black **AE** tail code was painted on a white diamond which was edged with red. The red rudder contained a vertical row of white stars.
(Flightleader)

Another one of the Diamondbacks' aircraft was photographed on the carrier USS INDEPENDENCE in 1975. Notice the absence of the red diamonds on the fuselage of this aircraft.
(Pickering)

Large red diamonds were later added to the fuselage of VF-102's aircraft as illustrated here. Barely noticeable on the top of the fuselage is the large white diamond that was edged in red.
(Flightleader)

F-4J, 155510, was being used by VF-102 as their CAG aircraft when this photograph was taken on July 11, 1975. The large red and white diamond on the top of the fuselage is barely visible. *(Centurion Enterprises)*

A different Phantom was being used by VF-102 as their CAG aircraft when this photograph was taken.

(Flightleader)

At left is still another Phantom that was used as VF-102's CAG aircraft. Notice the absence of the large fuselage diamonds on this aircraft. At right is a close-up view of the CAG markings painted on the white rudder. The diamonds were red, yellow, dark blue, green, orange, and red, from top to bottom. *(Both Flightleader)*

34

For the Bi-centennial year of 1976, VF-102 added a blue stripe inside the red and white diamond on the tail. The years **1776** and **1976** were positioned fore and aft of the **AG** tail code.

(Ostrowski)

Although the **AG** tail codes were retained, this photograph shows a change in carrier assignment. **USS DWIGHT D. EISENHOWER** was lettered in black on the bottom of the tail, and small red diamonds were painted on the white rudder.

(Flightleader Collection)

This aircraft was painted in an overall gloss gray scheme when it was photographed on October 14, 1978. Notice the carrier name **USS INDEPENDENCE** painted in black on the tail and the change to the **AE** tail code.

(Ostrowski)

By early 1980, all color had disappeared in VF-102's markings. This aircraft had dark gray markings on the light gray paint scheme.

(Flightleader)

VF-103 SLUGGERS

F-4J, 157309, carries the full color markings once used by VF-103. The large yellow arrow painted on the tail was edged with black.
(Flightleader Collection)

Even though F-4J, 155516, is shown here on the flight deck of the USS AMERICA, the carrier name **USS SARATOGA** was painted in black on the fuselage. Evidently the aircraft was "just visiting" AMERICA.
(Peacock)

One of the Sluggers' CAG aircraft was F-4J, 157279, which was photographed in August 1975. However, the aircraft did not carry special CAG markings except for the **200** modex.
(Grove)

A different CAG aircraft for VF-103 is seen in this photograph taken in 1976. Notice the Bi-centennial flag painted on the fuselage.
(Tripodi)

At left is an overall view of another one of VF-103's Phantoms that carried Bi-centennial markings. At right is a close-up view of the special red, white, and blue marking.
(Both Flightleader)

This all gray Phantom shows the addition of the black horizontal stripes that were painted on the tail.
(Flightleader)

Several changes are evident in this photograph which was taken of F-4J, 155754, in 1979. The squadron was changing to low visibility dark gray markings that were applied over the light gray paint scheme. The colorful yellow arrow had been retained on the tail, and the carrier name **USS SARA-TOGA** was located on the fuselage.
(Flightleader)

Even less color is visible on this aircraft than the one shown above. The large yellow arrow had been replaced with a small yellow arrow that is barely visible at the top of the fin cap. The **AC** tail code was staggered on the tail instead of being horizontal.
(Campbell)

VF-103 had transitioned to the tactical scheme by early 1982. The squadron was then assigned to the USS FOR-RESTAL and carried **AA** tail codes. A large outline of an arrow was on the tail in yellow and dark gray. (Grove)

This left side view of F-4J, 157245, illustrates the markings applied to that side of the aircraft. (Grove)

VF-142 GHOSTRIDERS

Although VF-142 is a Pacific Fleet squadron, it embarked on a deployment aboard USS AMERICA, which is a carrier assigned to the Atlantic Fleet. During this deployment, The Ghostriders carried their usual squadron markings, but changed to Atlantic Fleet tail codes. Codes used by the Atlantic Fleet begin with the letter **A**, while those used by the Pacific Fleet begin with an **N**. Therefore, it is unusual to see a squadron that is usually assigned to the Pacific Fleet using tail codes that begin with an **A**. F-4J, 155894, was assigned to VF-142 during that time period, and was painted in very colorful squadron markings when this photograph was taken on September 19, 1973. A large yellow stripe was painted from behind the cockpit to the tail, and the yellow bars painted on the white rudder were edged in black. The carrier name **USS AMERICA** was lettered in black on the yellow fuselage stripe. *(Flightleader Collection)*

This photograph was taken at NAS North Island, California, on September 6, 1974. The colorful yellow and white markings on the fuselage and tail were very attractive. *(Bergagnini)*

This right side view of the same Phantom illustrates the markings on that side of the aircraft. *(MAP)*

39

VF-143 PUKIN' DOGS

VF-143 is the sister squadron to VF-142, and they also deployed aboard the Atlantic Fleet carrier, USS AMERICA, and temporarily used **AJ** tail codes. F-4J, 155766, was photographed at NAS Miramar, California, on September 19, 1973. NAS Miramar is the shore base for all but two of the Pacific Fleet's fighter squadrons. The blue stripe across the fuselage contained **USS AMERICA** in black, and **VF-143** was in black above **NAVY**. A thin blue stripe was painted up the leading edge of the tail to the blue fin cap.

(Flightleader Collection)

F-4J, 155761, was assigned to VF-143 when this photograph was taken in 1974. The thin stripe that ran along the top of the fuselage and up the tail was dark blue. The squadron emblem on the fuselage was black.　　(MAP)

A left side view of another Phantom further illustrates the markings used by the Pukin' Dogs.　　(MAP)

40

VF-151 FIGHTING VIGILANTES

While VF-151 was also a Pacific Fleet squadron, it carried Atlantic Fleet tail codes of **AH** for a short time. Its shore base is NAF Atsugi, Japan. This photograph, taken in September 1970, shows F-4B, 151003, in the markings that were being used by Fighting Vigilantes at that time. Notice that the red color on the canopy rails extends along the black anti-glare shield and along the edge of the unusual black stripe to the front of the radome.   (Picciani Aircraft Slides)

Another one of VF-151's Phantoms that served with the Atlantic Fleet was 152267. The aircraft had black flashes painted across the yellow vertical tail and white rudder.
                                    (Flightleader Collection)

VF-171 ACES

In late 1977, the Bi-centennial markings used previously by VF-101 were still seen on some aircraft after the squadron was redesignated VF-171. However, a new squadron badge replaced the old Grim Reapers emblem used by VF-101.
(Flightleader)

At left is a view of the typical squadron markings used by VF-171, with the stylized **AD** tail code painted in black and edged in white. At right is a close-up view of the Aces' squadron badge. *(Both Flightleader)*

Another one of VF-171's Phantoms is illustrated in this left front view.
(Flightleader)

F-4J, 155558, is painted in the overall gray paint scheme but retains colorful markings.   (Flightleader Collection)

VF-171 had changed to low visibility markings by the time this photograph was taken of F-4J, 155868, in late 1981. All markings were in a contrasting dark gray over the light gull gray scheme.   (Kinzey)

F-4J, 157282, was marked with the **200** modex that would indicate that it was the commander's aircraft for VF-171. However, no other special markings were carried.   (Stewart)

VF-171 later painted some of their air-craft in the tactical scheme. F-4S, 155787, was one such example. All markings were in a dark or light con-trasting gray color, including the small **AD** tail code that is barely visible on the fin cap. (Flightleader)

Here is another one of the Aces' Phan-toms that was painted in the tactical scheme. (Flightleader)

A different style of **AD** tail code is illus-trated in this photograph of F-4S, 155528, which was taken in July 1983. All markings were in a dark charcoal gray color. (Flightleader Collection)

This Phantom was photographed operating on the deck of the USS AMERICA on November 11, 1983. (Kinzey Collection)

VF-171 (KEY WEST DETACHMENT)

Even after the squadron was redesignated, a Key West detachment was maintained to provide ACM training for the Atlantic Fleet. This F-4N, 152293, was one of the aircraft assigned to Key West, and it illustrates the markings used by VF-171KW.
(Flightleader)

VF-171KW also followed the trend to low visibility schemes and markings in the late 1970s. The only color still present on this Phantom was the VF-171KW badge on the fuselage of the aircraft.
(Ostrowski)

Although it was painted in the low visibility scheme, this Phantom still retained a red chevron on the tail. All other markings, including the stylized **AD** tail code, were in a dark contrasting gray color.
(Sides)

F-4S, 153873, is illustrated here in the tactical scheme in May 1983. Notice the slightly different stylized **AD** tail code.
(Spering/A.I.R.)

VF-201 RANGERS

VF-201 is one of the Naval Reserve fighter squadrons assigned to the Atlantic Fleet. Their CAG aircraft in 1977 was F-4N, 152244, and it was marked with the beautiful tail markings shown in this photograph. Notice the unusual nose modex **1000** on this aircraft.

(Rogers)

VF-201's Bi-centennial markings consisted of the **AF** tail codes being painted in blue on a white background, and a red chevron was on the front half of the tail. *(Spidle)*

This Phantom had a small red **76**, which was surrounded with blue stars, located on the bottom of the white rudder. *(Geer)*

VF-201 had a water-based light gray paint applied over their colorful markings during a training exercise. It almost looks as if it was applied with a broom. Some of the red on the tail can be seen bleeding through, although it isn't really very noticeable here.

(Huston)

This view of VF-201's flight line shows one aircraft in the squadron's usual markings, while all others have the temporary gray paint scheme.

(Flightleader Collection)

F-4N, 150442, further illustrates the temporary paint scheme used by the Rangers.

(Flightleader Collection)

VF-201 had started using a low visibility scheme by the time the photograph at left was taken of 150448 in July 1979. All markings, including the small **AF** tail codes, were in a contrasting dark gray color. At right is a close-up view of the small red zap found at the bottom of the splittler plate.

(Both Spidle)

Another example of VF-201's low visibility scheme is illustrated in this photograph. The minimal contrast between the grays made the markings very difficult to see. (Flightleader)

VF-201 brought some color back to their aircraft by the time this photograph was taken in June 1980. The red stripes on the tail and the black markings contrasted nicely against the overall gloss gray paint. The outline of the state of Texas was gray. (Grove)

This left rear view of F-4N, 151484, displays the colorful markings on the tail of the aircraft. Notice the small red star located inside the outline of the state of Texas to denote the location of NAS Dallas. (Rotramel)

*VF-201 also used the tactical scheme on some of their aircraft. F-4N, 150475, is one such example, and the only marking that is easy to read is the white **VF-201** on the fuselage.*   *(Flightleader Collection)*

The tactical scheme was used on VF-201's CAG aircraft, F-4S, 153909, which is shown here as it taxied out for a flight. Notice the light gray color used for the state of Texas on the tail.
(Grove)

Another tactical scheme is illustrated in this photograph of F-4S, 153826.
(Grove)

VF-202 SUPERHEATS

VF-202 is the other Naval Reserve fighter squadron assigned to the Atlantic Fleet. F-4N, 151463, is illustrated here with the colorful tail markings that this squadron used in the late 1970s. *(Spidle)*

This close-up of the splitter plate of 151463 provides a good look at the eight black and two white F-15 kill markings painted there. The black markings indicate confirmed kills, while the white markings are for probables that were scored in mock aerial combat with F-15s stationed at Holloman Air Force Base, New Mexico. The pilot of this aircraft was either very good, or the F-15 pilots had a bad day! In fairness, it should be noted that VF-202 had been flying the Phantom for a number of years, and Holloman's pilots had just received their F-15s when this air combat training took place. *(Spidle)*

This close-up view shows the F-15 kill markings painted on F-4N, 153056. An overall view of this aircraft is shown below. *(Spidle)*

F-4N, 153056, also displayed eight black F-15 kills and one white probable on its splitter plate. We would have loved to listen to the war stories told at the bar after these flights! *(Spidle)*

Another Phantom from VF-202 that carried F-15 kill markings was 152277. This photograph was taken at NAS Dallas, Texas, on November 11, 1978. *(Spidle)*

*This close-up of 152277's splitter plate shows the eight black and two white F-15 kill markings in good detail. Notice the name **ZIGGY** painted inside the nose wheel door.* *(Spidle)*

This close-up is of the splitter plate on F-4N, 150492. It only displays six kills. An overall view of this aircraft is shown below. *(Spidle)*

The right side of 150492 is shown in this photograph. The Texas state flag on the rudder was a standard marking used by VF-202 on their aircraft. *(Spidle)*

This Phantom carried the CAG markings for VF-202. These markings were in the form of multi-colored stars on the tail.
(GB Aircraft Slides)

This Phantom was painted in the overall glossy gray scheme. The yellow band made a nice contrast on the light gray fuselage. *(Kinzey)*

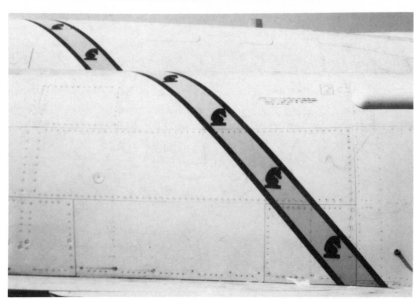

*At left is a closer look at the yellow and black fuselage band. At right is a view of the black and yellow **AF** code on the wing.*
(Both Kinzey)

The Superheats had started using white for the **VF-202, AF** tail codes, the modex, and **NAVY** when this photograph was taken on July 13, 1980. By this time the fuselage band had also disappeared from the aircraft.

(Flightleader)

The left side of F-4N, 150492, is shown in this photograph that was taken as the aircraft taxied out for departure.
(Flightleader)

VF-202 experimented with an unusual angular type of paint scheme on some of their aircraft in 1984. F-4S, 153904, was one of the aircraft that was painted in that scheme. The squadron's markings on the rudder are still there, but are very difficult to see.

(Grove)

VF-202 also had some aircraft painted in the overall gray scheme. This one had colorful markings on the rudder, and the results of spot painting to change previous colorful markings to ones with low visibility can clearly be seen. A yellow band is painted around the travel pod.

(Flightleader)

F-4N, 152307, was painted in the overall light gull gray scheme with darker contrasting gray markings.

(Flightleader Collection)

This Phantom had a two-tone tactical paint scheme with contrasting gray markings. The Texas flag on the rudder was also painted in various shades of gray.

(Flightleader Collection)

This aircraft is painted in an overall gray that appears to be one of the colors used in the tactical scheme. Notice that it is a darker and bluer shade of gray than that seen on the tail of the aircraft parked next to it.

(Flightleader Collection)

At left is an overall view of one of the Superheats' Phantoms that is painted in the two-tone tactical scheme. Even though this aircraft carries the **200** modex, there are no special CAG markings. At right is a closer look at the tail markings.
(Both Flightleader)

F-4S, 155765, had a similar two-tone tactical scheme, however the shades of gray appear to be lighter. There seems to have been little in the way of adherence to FS numbers for shades of paint used in many of the units. At left is a look at the complete right side of the aircraft. At right is a close-up of the markings painted on the tail. (Both Flightleader)

VAQ-33 HUNTERS

F-4B, 149461, was operated by VAQ-33 at the time this photograph was taken on September 25, 1976. At left is an overall view of the right side of this aircraft. At right is a closer view of the red squadron emblem on the tail. The lightning bolt was yellow.

(Left Leslie, right Flightleader)

VAQ-33 also operated the F-4J, as evidenced by this photograph taken in April 1977. The markings were the same as seen in the photograph above. The 10 modex on the nose was painted black and shadowed in red.

(Flightleader)

This Phantom had been designated an EF-4J by VAQ-33. The 11 modex on the nose was red and edged with black.

(Grove)

NADC

One of the F-4Bs operated by the Naval Air Development Center at NAF Warminister, Pennsylvania, is shown in this photograph that was taken as the plane was landing. The yellow emblem on the tail was on a dark blue disc, and had **NADC** lettered in red.
(Picciani Aircraft Slides)

One of the first QF-4Bs converted for the Navy was photographed in August 1972. The aircraft was painted an over-all red-orange.
(Picciani Aircraft Slides)

NADC had changed their markings by 1975. This photo illustrates the new markings on its tail.   (Stewart)

NATF

BuNo. 148265 was an F-4A that was assigned to the Naval Air Test Facility at NAS Lakehurst, New Jersey, when this photograph was taken on May 28, 1968. The aircraft had black and yellow stripes painted on the orange tail, with the number **4** and **NATF** being lettered in black. *(Flightleader Collection)*

YF-4J, 151497, was assigned to the Naval Air Test Facility when this photograph was taken in 1973. The aircraft had **NATF 7** in black on the yellow triangle. *(MAP)*

NATF's markings had been changed by the time this photograph of 151497 was taken in May 1977. At left is an overall view of the left side of the aircraft, while at right is a close-up view of the new markings. The red chevron was painted on a white disc that was edged in red. **NATF** and **LAKEHURST** were painted in black on the disc.

(Both Flightleader Collection)

NATC
FLIGHT TEST DIRECTORATE

This early F-4A, 143388, was a test aircraft assigned to the Naval Air Test Center, NAS Patuxent River, Maryland. It was photographed in May 1959 just after completing a flight.　(Picciani Aircraft Slides)

F-4G, 150625, was also assigned to NATC when it was photographed on July 23, 1960. The F-4G designation used for a short time by the Navy should not be confused with the F-4G Wild Weasel aircraft used by the Air Force. These F-4Gs were modified F-4Bs used to evaluate an automatic carrier landing system. They were later restored to their original F-4B configuration. This aircraft had a white chevron painted on the tail to designate it as a flight test aircraft.

(Picciani Aircraft Slides)

This F-4J was another Phantom that was assigned to NATC in mid-1971. The tail and end of the wing panels were painted international orange.

(Picciani Aircraft Slides)

WEAPONS TEST DIRECTORATE

F-4A, 145309, was also assigned to NATC as a test aircraft. The large **W** painted on the tail in orange indicated that it was used for weapons testing. There were orange stripes painted along the fuselage and on the upper portion of the tail.

(Picciani Aircraft Slides)

Another weapons test aircraft was F-4B, 150415, which was photographed on May 16, 1969. An orange **W** was also painted on the tail of this aircraft.
(Picciani Aircraft Slides)

*A change in NATC markings is evident in this photograph of 150415 that was taken in 1970. The aircraft had orange tail and wing panels, and the large **W** was painted white.*
(Picciani Aircraft Slides)

SYSTEMS TEST DIRECTORATE

F-4A, 146819, was assigned to systems testing at NATC when photographed in May 1965. Notice the nicely shadowed S painted in gold on the tail.
(Picciani Aircraft Slides)

This F-4B was also operated by NATC and carried the markings of the Systems Test Directorate. The black stylized S was outlined in yellow and located on the orange tail surface.
(Flightleader Collection)

F-4J, 153077, displays slightly different markings for the Systems Test Directorate. The large stylized S painted on the orange tail was black and edged in white.

(Centurion Enterprises)

UNIFIED DIRECTORATES

One of the first Phantoms modified to the F-4S configuration was 155565. The aircraft was tested by NATC and carried their emblem at the top of the tail. Notice the special red, blue, and yellow Phantom "spook" markings on the tail and centerline tank.

(Ostrowski)

At left is a closer look at the NATC emblem and spook on the right side of the tail. At right is the opposite side, which carried the Strike Aircraft Test badge and the spook. (Flightleader Collection)

This former Blue Angels aircraft was operated by NATC with the large number removed from the tail and replaced with the NATC badge. The words **BLUE ANGELS** have been removed from the aircraft, and **NAVAL AIR TEST CENTER** has been added to the nose. The modex **839** has been added to the nose, and the national insignia has been painted on the intakes. (Flightleader)

The right side of 153839 is shown here. (Flightleader)

Another change in paint schemes and markings for NATC is seen in these photographs that are dated September 9, 1977. The overall view at left shows the unusual test boom attached to the nose of the aircraft. At right is a close-up view of the markings on the tail.
(Both Flightleader)

This overall gray Phantom shows the appearance of the *7T* tail code that NATC started using on their aircraft by the early 1980s. (Flightleader)

This view of F-4S, 157286, illustrates the markings painted on the left side of the aircraft. (Ostrowski)

BLUE ANGELS

Although entire books have been dedicated to the aircraft and markings used by the Blue Angels, this book would not be complete without a brief look at the F-4Js flown by Navy's famous flight demonstration team that is home-based at NAS Pensacola, Florida. This close formation is typical of their flying demonstrations, and reveals some of the team's markings that were used on the F-4Js.

(Flightleader)

Like other aircraft flown by the Blues, the F-4Js were painted the special glossy blue color that is generally known as "Blue Angels Blue." Markings are a bright deep yellow. This overview of Phantoms 2 and 3 further illustrates the markings on the aircraft.

(Flightleader)

The line-up of the Blue Angels' aircraft was an impressive sight that captured the hearts of young and old alike. This flight demonstration team is one of the most effective recruiting and public relations tools that the Navy has.

(Flightleader)